100
THINGS TO DO IN
MINNESOTA
BEFORE YOU
DIE

MW00533472

#10 - August Schell's
A beer for all seasons!

Julio Jc Larso

An eagle overlooking the Mississippi River

100

THINGS TO DO IN

MINNESOTA

BEFORE YOU

DIE

• •

JULIE JO LARSON

REEDY PRESS

Copyright © 2023 by Reedy Press, LLC
Reedy Press
PO Box 5131
St. Louis, MO 63139, USA
www.reedypress.com

Permissions may be sought directly from Reedy Press at the above mailing address or via our website at www.reedypress.com.

Library of Congress Control Number: 2022949242

ISBN: 9781681064253

Design by Jill Halpin

All photos are by the author unless otherwise noted.

Printed in the United States of America
23 24 25 26 27   5 4 3 2 1

DEDICATION

100 Things to Do in Minnesota Before You Die is dedicated to all who call Minnesota home and the many visitors who seek what lies just beyond the river bend, over the next hill, through the big woods, or on the next street corner.

Crossing Arts Alliance across from Fancy Pants Chocolate (page 20)

CONTENTS

• •

Music and Entertainment

• •

• •

Culture and History

• •

• •

PREFACE

For my second contribution to Reedy Press's *100 Things to Do* series, I was given the opportunity to stray a bit from the formula and chose to broaden my scope to the entire state of Minnesota. With worn mukluks on my feet and a walking stick in hand, I traveled from our northern wilderness to our metropolitan cities and onward to our southern prairie in search of "Things."

The Minnesota most people imagine is the home of 10,000 lakes, four seasons, lush forestland, fertile farms, and uncharted wilderness. The Minnesota I know also has award-winning restaurants, innovative medical facilities, grand entertainment establishments, national sporting teams, and, of course, the pinnacle of USA shopping: the Mall of America.

Whether you live here 12 months a year or are visiting for the first time, you will discover new adventures waiting for you in every section of this book. So, grab your copy of *100 Things to Do in Minnesota Before You Die* and your favorite travel companion because I just added a few more "Things" to your bucket list.

since 1934

DOMEIERS

A trip to
Domeier's
is like a trip to the
old country

Old World Store

STOCKED WITH THE SAME MERCHANDISE
FOUND IN THE SHOPS OF

Germany

Domeier's in New Ulm (page 108)

ACKNOWLEDGMENTS

I am eternally grateful for my adult children, Alex, Sorina, Morgan, and Josh, who take the time to savor the many journeys that lead to great destinations. Stephen, may you remember reaching every destination, even if you thought we dillydallied too much. To Patricia, Peggy, Maria, Bones, Nancy, family, coworkers, and friends: thank you for your encouragement! To Krista Soukup, Bradley Miller, Karin Nelson, Leigh Melby, Maggie Fuller, Camp Candace authors, instructor extraordinaire Sheila O'Connor, and the fine folks at Reedy Press: thank you for sharing your expertise. And to everyone who patiently listened to me describe the latest "Thing" I discovered: there are more things to come!

Breakfast at Wings Airport Café (page 2)

FOOD
AND DRINK

FLY IN OR DRIVE
TO WINGS AIRPORT CAFÉ

A great meal and a fun view await you at Wings Airport Café located just outside of Brainerd. Since 2014, Mark Nesham's fresh-from-scratch breakfasts, lunches, and desserts tantalize taste buds. Mouthwatering caramel rolls are the perfect start to any breakfast. Follow up your sweet treat with wild rice pancakes topped with real blueberries or a full-size breakfast with just-baked bread, thick-sliced bacon, hash browns, made-your-way eggs, and a bottomless cup of hot coffee. Daily breakfast and lunch specials provide ample opportunity to try something new.

Hold on to your napkin though. As you dine, small aircraft land, refuel, and take off just yards from your table. Children and adults love watching the changing view. If you're lucky, Kimmy will serve your meal and entertain you with her charm and humor. Great food, interesting views, and fantastic service are waiting for you at Wings Airport Café.

16384 Airport Rd., Ste. #7, Brainerd, 218-828-0206
wingsairportcafe.com

TIP

During the summer, sports figures, Blackhawks, and entertainers are often guests at Wings. Keep your eyes open and your cell phone camera ready!

ENJOY THE IGLOO BAR
AT ZIPPEL BAY

Beautiful, frozen Lake of the Woods is proof that Minnesotans are hardy and really do enjoy all four seasons. Although there are several noteworthy resorts on this lake, each with their own bar, the Igloo Bar stands out as the most unique. Most years, it rests on Zippel Bay, just out from Zippel Bay Resort. From hard freeze until the ice softens, trucks and snowmobiles travel a plowed ice road to reach this licensed mobile food court.

It's a Northern Minnesota winter destination complete with heated porta potties shaped like mini igloos, hot bar food, cold beverages, and big-screen TVs. One of the favorite activities is fishing in a frozen, rented hole while sipping a cold beer from a barstool. It's worth the trip to catch a walleye in the Igloo Bar in January!

State Hwy. 11, Baudette, 800-382-3474
lakeofthewoodsmn.com

SAVOR
PREMIUM ICE CREAM

Eating ice cream 12 months a year is natural for native Minnesotans. My first job in the 1980s was working at Dannheim's Kuhstall, a dairy in New Ulm that made its own ice cream every Saturday. Although Dannheim's closed some years ago, premium ice cream is still available in small towns across the state.

Another Time Ice Cream Parlor in Lanesboro is hard to miss with its bright, pink sherbet–colored exterior. The ice cream window is full of visitors all summer long. Located on the Root River State Trail, bikers young and not-so-young line up for butter pecan waffle cones and other cool treats.

In Crosby, Victual serves Midnight ice cream each winter. The combination of black licorice and orange liqueur hangs on your taste buds long after your last bite. Victual is open all year and sells meats, cheeses, teas, Northwoods souvenirs, and a variety of other items.

Another Time Ice Cream Parlor
100 Parkway Ave. N, Lanesboro, 507-467-3556
anothertimeicecream.com

Victual
124 W Main St., Crosby, 218-545-1000
shopvictual.com

GRAB BARBECUE
AT WILBUR'S ON WALKER BAY

Wandering through Walker on a warm July afternoon? Wilbur's restaurant/sports bar is the hot spot for tender and juicy barbecue, cold soda, and a great selection of beer. Sit on the street-side patio and watch the steady flow of people walking by. If you need a break from "peopling," a flight of stairs leads you to an outdoor dining area surrounded by flower gardens, and a small stage where bands play on summer weekends. This outdoor area entices patrons to slow down and enjoy the food, music, and nature.

My standard order is the Pig Pen with a side of crunchy tater tots. A toasted bun is loaded with house-smoked pulled pork and shaved ham, drizzled with flavorful barbecue sauce, and topped with a sizeable onion ring and sriracha coleslaw. The flavors tastefully blend together. Mmm.

101 5th St., Walker, 218-547-4777
facebook.com/wilbursonwalkerbay

ENJOY A PATIO LUNCH
AT SAGE ON LAUREL

Sage on Laurel is located in historic downtown Brainerd. The menu includes American classics and flavors from around the world. From locally supplied beef burgers to spring rolls to flavorful baked bruschetta, the ever-changing menu offers something for every appetite. In addition to locally farm-grown ingredients, Sage on Laurel grows their own herbs on their patio garden in summer.

In warm months, the outdoor patio overlooks some of the downtown's oldest buildings. It's a great lunch area for small children. The tastefully renovated interior dining area is the perfect setting for meetings, wedding showers, and book clubs. From beautiful hardwood floors to well-preserved tin ceiling tiles, the historic charm of the building shines through. History, great architecture, and savory foods make Sage on Laurel an area favorite.

606 Laurel St., Brainerd, 218-454-7243
sageonlaurel.com

MEET THE USA 2022 BARTENDER OF THE YEAR
AT SPOON AND STABLE

Spoon and Stable's creator is Chef Gavin Kaysen, a James Beard Award–winning chef. The restaurant was a 2015 James Beard finalist for Best New Restaurant. The food is French inspired, which suits the setting, a rustic vintage carriage house building. Exquisite food at Spoon and Stable is complemented by the cocktails created by Jessi Pollak. Pollak holds the distinction of earning the title 2022 USA Bartender of the Year.

Pollak used speed, creativity, fresh ingredients, and bar theatrics to earn the honor. Her cocktail creations include the freshest vegetables, fruits, and spirits. Pollak's Jungle Bird is garnished with pineapple fronds and tastes as scrumptious as it looks. She'll tell you a tale as she mixes your beverage and keeps the whole bar entertained. Reservations are required well in advance.

211 N 1st St., Minneapolis, 612-224-9850
spoonandstable.com

TRY A SLICE OF PIE
AT RAPIDAN DAM STORE

Rapidan Dam Store is open May 1 through October 31 and as the name suggests, it is located by an actual dam. The family-owned café serves burgers, fries, onion rings, and pie! On any given day, there are close to a dozen different pie choices. From banana cream to strawberry rhubarb, Rapidan Dam has a different pie for every day of the week. By the slice, or by the pie, your taste buds will thank you.

This secluded café is located near Mankato. With its old-fashioned Texaco gas pump and quaint interior, it's a nice change from the chain restaurants in town. Great service is one reason locals return time after time. Take a stretch after your meal and view the dam as water rushes through. It will take you back to simpler times.

54116 Glory Ln., Mankato, 507-546-9997

EXPERIENCE
THE RAPID RIVER LOGGING CAMP

In the 1800s, loggers spent months at a time in logging camps such as the Rapid River Logging Camp. Cutting down virgin white pine created quite the appetite. Although there is no active logging on-site, visitors can learn about the logging era through the interactive activities. Walk the trails, check out the equipment and saws, feed the chickens, and wander through the Foreman's Shack gift shack. The gift shop is well stocked with snacks and trinkets for the children.

With all those steps logged, you'll be ready for an "all-you-can-eat, family-style meal." The dinner hall is set up with red-checkered oilcloth, metal plates, and tin cups. Boots, saw blades, and smaller logging tools make for interesting mealtime conversation. Bring your appetite because the food is hearty!

15073 County Rd. 18, Park Rapids, 218-732-3444
rapidriverloggingcamp.com

TASTE THE WORLD
AT MIDTOWN GLOBAL MARKET

The Midtown Global Market offers the world at your fingertips. Each time I visit, there are new food and retail vendors. It is a place to purchase groceries, enjoy a prepared meal, or shop for hard-to-find ingredients. It is a big asset to the community and the city because it brings a wide assortment of cultures together. However, food and retail are just part of the market.

The market offers visitors the opportunity to learn about our neighbors, their culture, and history. Dance lessons, musical events, virtual cooking lessons, and special events add to the energy at the Midtown Global Market.

The Eastlake Craft Brewery is a fun stop in the summer; their outdoor patio is a great place to connect with friends. Los Ocampo creates authentic Mexican food using fresh ingredients and family recipes. There are so many food choices; multiple visits are in order.

920 E Lake St., Minneapolis, 612-872-4140
midtownglobalmarket.org

SIP COLD BEER
AT AUGUST SCHELL
BREWING COMPANY

August Schell was one of the cofounders of New Ulm. In 1860, the Schell's Brewery was built, mostly because August couldn't find good beer to whet his whistle. He and Jacob Bernhardt (the brewmaster) built their brewery along the Cottonwood River, where the water was cool and clean. The brewery survived the Dakota War of 1862 and now claims the title of second-oldest brewery in Minnesota.

The beautiful Schell's Mansion was built in 1885 and is still a highlight of a visit to the brewery. In addition to the gift shop and beautiful gardens, visitors can stroll the grounds where they might see a peacock or spot the deer that live on-site. Let's face it, the highlight of a tour is participating in the beer sampling and a visit to the Schell's Bier Halle. What began with one beer has morphed into a large selection of award-winning beer, including Schell's Oktoberfest.

1860 Schell Rd., New Ulm, 800-770-5020
schellsbrewery.com

TIP

In 2002, Schell's acquired Grain Belt Beer. Craft beers are now added to the production line yearly. Visit their website for the newest beer options!

STOP FOR CARAMEL ROLLS AND MORE
AT THE MALMO MARKET

The Malmo Market has been a family stop for us since the 1980s. The large chicken statue pays tribute to their great-tasting broasted chicken. Chicken is just one of the many favorites at Malmo Market. No stop to the cabin or Mille Lacs Lake is complete without a double-scoop waffle cone. Rich and creamy, the ice cream flavors are too numerous to list. I take advantage of the new flavors every stop.

New owners bought this treasured store in the summer of 2022. The first thing customers asked was, "What about the caramel rolls?" Have no fear, the caramel rolls will continue to be baked fresh daily along with all the other favorites. In addition to chicken, ice cream, and caramel rolls, there is a grocery store, hardware section, boat and outdoor supplies, and gasoline.

32060 220th St., Aitkin, 320-684-2295

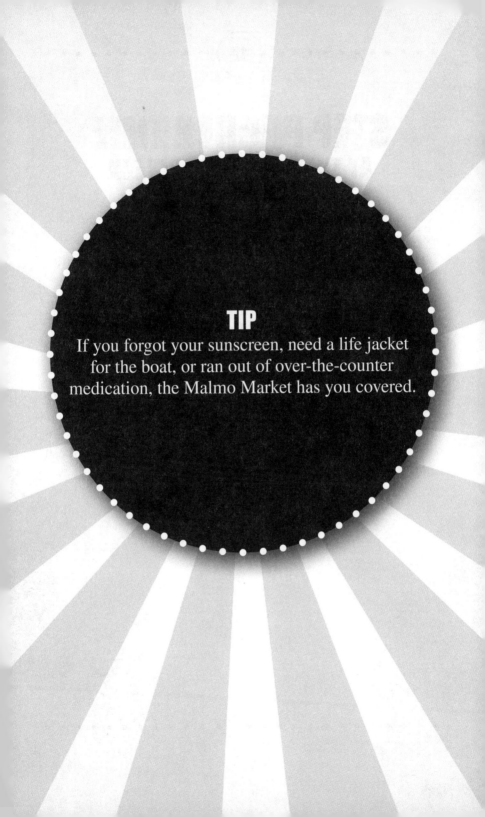

TIP

If you forgot your sunscreen, need a life jacket for the boat, or ran out of over-the-counter medication, the Malmo Market has you covered.

STEP BACK IN TIME
AT THE COUNTRY DRIVE IN

This stop was one I hadn't heard of before. For over 30 years, the Country Drive In has been serving folks in Southern Minnesota buckets and buckets of chicken and other American favorites with real drive-in service. Yes, you can have your tray attached to the side of your car. It's a family business where siblings often take over for older siblings when they head off to college. They only serve during the summer months, so keep an eye on the calendar.

Reviews compare the Country Drive In to the 1950s classic malt shops because the malts are made with real ice cream and served with a smile. The food is made to order and you can eat inside if you choose to. Make note though, they accept only cash and checks, no credit or debit cards. Just like in the '50s.

802 5th St. W, Winthrop, 507-647-5303

SAVOR DINNER
AT OWAMNI BY THE SIOUX CHEF

This full-service restaurant sits on the bank of the Mississippi River in Minneapolis inside the Water Works Pavilion in Mill Ruins Park. Sean Sherman, the Sioux Chef, was recently awarded a James Beard Award. He and Dana Thompson offer the true flavors of North American food. Indigenous restaurants are not common in Minnesota, so we are excited to highlight Owamni. The great meals begin with ingredients purchased from Indigenous producers, including wild rice, fresh berries, and local vegetables. Food offerings are naturally gluten free, dairy free, cane sugar free, soy free, and pork free in keeping with traditional Indigenous cooking.

Fresh fish, duck, bison, and turkey are prepared with an assortment of fresh greens, beans, and vegetables. I am looking forward to enjoying cedar and maple baked beans with a mug of cider on their outdoor patio in the summer. Perhaps I'll see you there!

420 1st St. S, Minneapolis, 612-242-9700
owamni.com

CHOOSE CHEESE
AT GATOR'S GRILLED CHEESE EMPORIUM

Without a doubt, Gator's Grilled Cheese Emporium is focused on grilled cheese sandwiches and mac and cheese. Their traditional sandwiches are served with kettle chips, and for a fee, you can add that must-have bowl of tomato soup—what else would you dip your sandwich in? Gator's understands the way Minnesotans eat their favorite American sandwich. If you're really hungry, you can even add a side of mac and cheese. Or, you can order the Bacon Mac and Cheese Sandwich and have all your favorite food items between two slices of multigrain bread. You only live once! Gator's makes a great variety of breakfast items, perfect to fuel a day of shopping.

This "Thing" will take a bit of planning because Gator's is currently closed on Wednesdays and Thursdays. Check ahead to make sure their days of service haven't changed because cheese lovers will want to satisfy their cravings.

955 E Sheridan St., Ely, 218-365-7348
gatorsinely.com

TREAT YOURSELF
TO MINNESOTA GROWN
FRUITS AND VEGETABLES

Nothing beats Minnesota-grown fresh fruits and vegetables. From late spring until past frost, we grow some of the tastiest. Many farmers are extending their growing season using tunnel farming and heaters. With this technology, tomatoes are naturally ripening into November. Think of the salads and salsa we can make.

Minnesota Grown is a statewide partnership between the Minnesota Department of Agriculture and Minnesota producers of specialty crops, flowers, eggs, and livestock. The Minnesota Grown website allows visitors to search for summer farmer markets and winter markets. It also offers recipes and a wholesale directory. Instead of searching for fresh farmers markets across the state, look for "Minnesota Grown" symbols next to your favorite farm and garden producers.

651-201-6140
minnesotagrown.com

SATISFY YOUR SWEET TOOTH
AT MINNESOTA CANDY AND CHOCOLATE STORES

Need to satisfy a sweet tooth? You are in luck! Minnesota is home to great candy and chocolate stores. In the Northwoods, Fancy Pants Chocolates is home to chocolate creations made by chocolatier Nancy Williams. Williams has been perfecting her three dozen–plus creations since 2002. Dark-chocolate-covered cherries and caramel pecan clusters are my favorites. If you have a favorite, order ahead because her shelves empty quickly and chocoholics get cranky without chocolate.

If chocolate isn't your thing, perhaps a trip to Minnesota's Largest Candy Store is in order. This candy store is also called Jim's Apple Farm. You can't miss the yellow barn. From May through November, candy lovers of all ages flock to the candy store. In addition to all your favorite candy, they include the world's largest selection of soda, many varieties of popcorn, baked goods, and more. The shelves are well organized and displays are fun and brightly colored. Bring cash or checks; no plastic is accepted.

Fancy Pants Chocolates
704 Laurel St., Brainerd, 218-828-7844
fancypantschocolates.com

Minnesota's Largest Candy Store
20430 Johnson Memorial Dr., Jordan, 952-492-6380
minnesotaslargestcandystore.business.site

TIP
Sweetly Kismet Candy Store is Northern
Minnesota's largest candy store. They also
offer soda pop, gifts, and more!

11707 Hwy. 210, Carlton

CHOOSE CHICKEN
AT CARL'S CORNER

My sister introduced me to Carl's Corner. It was packed with locals ordering tons of never-frozen broasted chicken. So naturally, I ordered what the locals were enjoying. I was not disappointed. The skin was crispy and the chicken was moist. The coleslaw, a special blend with vinegar, was not too sweet, not too sour. The servings were large, so we had plenty for a late-night snack. My family also recommended the pizza served with pitchers of cold beer. Maybe next time.

Carl's Corner is located in downtown Essig, a small town with a population of 56. Customers come from 60 miles or more to enjoy an evening meal. From my experience, avoid the 6 to 7 p.m. rush. You can reserve a table online. The sunsets in that area are amazing due to the lack of trees and hills. You can watch the colors change as you sip a cold beer and grab that last bite of chicken.

21378 1st St., Essig, 507-354-4241

GRAB LUNCH
AT PEDAL PUSHERS CAFÉ

Located in beautiful Lanesboro, Pedal Pushers Café serves everything from classics to Korean-style pork bowls, Norwegian meatballs, and bison burgers. They offer vegan, vegetarian, and gluten-free options, making this a café for the entire family. They serve Minnesota beers on tap and a selection of hard ciders and wine. For dessert, try the Triple Berry Panna Cotta or a brownie sundae.

Pedal Pushers Café has both indoor and outdoor tables. Located just a few blocks from the Root River State Trail, it's a hot spot for bikers, in-line skaters, and hikers. After enjoying a fun meal at Pedal Pushers Café, you can rent a canoe or kayak from a local outfitter and enjoy the river. Lanesboro's downtown area is historic and a neat place to wander through.

121 Parkway Ave. N, Lanesboro, 507-467-1050
pedalpusherscafe.com

ADD A MINNESOTA WINE
TO YOUR DINNER

Bet you weren't expecting this "Thing." However, Minnesota Wineries produce award-winning wines. In addition to wonderful wines, wineries also offer fun extras such as art demonstrations, date nights, wine tours, and live music events. It's impossible to include all of Minnesota's wineries, so I chose just a few.

In Southern Minnesota, Morgan Creek Vineyards and Winery produces Nova, a semisweet red that is great for sipping. Morgan Creek has food offerings that are European-inspired, tours, yoga and brunch specials, live music, and visiting media artist exhibits.

Central Minnesota's Dennis Drummond Wine Company has a bistro and event room perfect for special occasions. Their House Rosé wine is award winning and one of my favorites. On weekends, visitors can tap their toes and listen to local bands.

Traveling to Bemidji? Forestedge Winery is set in the lush Northwoods. The winery is surrounded by trees, chickens, and nature. The Babe Blue is a semisweet wine that combines blueberry and white cranberry wines. It's light and crisp, served best chilled.

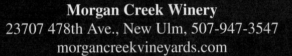

Morgan Creek Winery
23707 478th Ave., New Ulm, 507-947-3547
morgancreekvineyards.com

Dennis Drummond Wine Company
11919 Thiesse Rd., Brainerd, 218-454-3392
ddwco.com

Forestedge Winery
35295 MN-64, Laporte, 218-224-3535
forestedgewinery.com

SAMPLE CRAFT BEER
AT SMALL-TOWN BREWERIES

Do you cheer for craft beer? As of summer of 2022, there were over 200 craft breweries in Minnesota, placing us number 13 in the nation. We have new craft breweries opening yearly; each has its own flair. Axe throwing, indoor and outdoor music, art demonstrations, and clever games are abundant extras.

Some favorite craft breweries include Junkyard Brewing Company in Moorhead. Their double IPAs, juicy fruited sours, and pastry stouts impress judges.

BlackStack Brewing is a metro brewery that is full of Minnesota nice. Wild Times is a golden sour with passionfruit, and a favorite of many patrons.

Go north, way north, to Castle Danger Brewery. Located in Two Harbors, Castle Danger is off the beaten path, and well worth the trip. My daughter enjoys the drive from Duluth to Two Harbors. The scenic route offers great views of Lake Superior. Castle Danger is well known for its ales, which seem to capture Lake Superior in every glass.

TIP

What's the best way to find a small-town brewery? Check the local chamber of commerce website or go to mncraftbrew.org.

Junkyard Brewing Company
1416 1st Ave. N, Moorhead, 701-936-5545
junkyardbeer.com

BlackStack Brewing
755 Prior Ave. N, Saint Paul, 651-808-0747
blackstackbrewing.com

Castle Danger Brewery
17 7th St., Two Harbors, 218-834-5800
castledangerbrewery.com

TASTE GERMANY
AT THE BLACK FOREST INN

The Black Forest Inn has been around so long that multiple generations of my family have enjoyed a cold beer with our sauerbraten. Founded in 1965, it has been a Minneapolis favorite. The menu includes all the classic German food I grew up with including German potato salad with real apple cider vinegar. I also saw a few menu items I didn't recognize such as fried cabbage. A biergarten and great bar area compliment the restaurant. All three have the traditional German atmosphere and room for friends to gather.

If you are in the metro in October, try the German festival Oktoberfest, which began as a wedding festival in 1810. True to tradition, the Black Forest Inn celebrates Oktoberfest with music, dancing, feathers, great food, and yes, a little beer.

1 E 26th St., Minneapolis, 612-872-0812
blackforestinnmpls.com

ENJOY THE VIEW
AT RUSTIC INN CAFÉ

After a stop at the Castle Danger Brewery, food might be in order. The Rustic Inn Café is open 12 months a year and serves gluten-free, vegetarian, and vegan menu items. Fresh Lake Superior fish is a menu favorite as are the homemade soups on chilly days when the wind blows off the lake. If you call ahead, you can do a pie check and save your favorite for the trip. The relaxed atmosphere is perfect before hitting the beaches of Lake Superior.

After your meal and dessert, continue north for a few miles. The views from this section of the shoreline are beautiful. On calm days, the lake resembles glass. But take warning, riptide warnings can be issued for Lake Superior when the winds blow too strong. The water is often too cold to swim in without a wet suit. The beach is a prime agate-hunting zone.

2773 Hwy. 61, Two Harbors, 218-834-2488
rusticinn.cafe

SIP CIDER
AT BATTLE LAKE'S 1910 SIP HOUSE

Wineries, breweries, and cider houses. Minnesotans love their adult beverages. The 1910 Sip House is located in the western part of the state on Ethyl Lake and specializes in small-batch craft cider. It all starts with fresh apples and then moves on to fermentation, which begins less than two days later. From there the process varies a bit. One interesting note is that the base for all their hard ciders is their Ethyl's Dry Cider. It is created by combining Honeycrisp, Sweet Tango, and Zestar apples, all grown in Minnesota.

On select summer evenings, guests can sip cider by the firepit and listen to a band from the 1910 Sip House's Summer Music lineup. The music and friendly atmosphere might entice you to try a glass of Pickledilly (infused with homemade dill pickle) or one of their special Cider Cocktails of the Week such as a Mud Season (salted caramel and coconut).

41714 Foursquare Rd., Battle Lake, 303-506-0027
1910siphouse.com

CHOMP ON AN APPLE
AT WHISTLING WELL FARM

Hastings has a longer growing season than Central or Northern Minnesota, so it's a great place to grow apples. Since 1972, Whistling Well Farm has been celebrating fall with the apple harvest. Not all apples are created equal. Some are great for pies but are not sweet enough for eating. Others are great for eating but too soft for pies. Luckily the staff at the farm know their apples. They'll help visitors pick the right apples for their chomping desires. A few of the fan favorites include Haralson, Honeycrisp, First Kiss, and Sweet Tango.

Pumpkins are another good indicator that fall is upon us. Shortly after apple season begins, Whistling Well Farm gets decked out for fall with pumpkin displays and potted mums. When the autumn wind hits their well just right, it whispers a little. Coins and bills thrown into the well are donated with a dollar-for-dollar match to the University of Minnesota Masonic Children's Hospital Nurses Fund.

8973 St. Croix Trail S, Hastings, 651-998-0301
whistlingwellfarm.com

BITE INTO
SPECIALTY PIZZA

Poor Gary's Pizza in downtown Moose Lake is a mom-and-pop joint where small-town atmosphere meets big-pizza taste. Wild rice, one of Minnesota's favorite grains, partners with tender chicken, real mozzarella cheese, and a creamy white sauce and is placed on a crispy, thin crust. Chicken wild rice pizza is a Northwoods favorite.

Log Cabin Pizza in Browerville is an upbeat, small-town pizza shop, with super fresh topping combinations. Take Grandma's Special: Alfredo sauce, tender chicken, broccoli, and mushrooms. Or the Chicken Cordon Blue with Canadian bacon, chicken, and that tasty Alfredo sauce. They have classic pizzas and build-your-own if you prefer.

Happy Joe's Pizza and Ice Cream has two Minnesota locations. Both offer sandwiches, pasta, salads, and pizza. Their Taco Joe Pizza is amazing! Refried bean sauce, taco-seasoned beef, sausage, and the basic toppings. Once the pizza comes out of the oven, tomato, lettuce, and crushed taco chips are added. Sour cream and taco sauce come on the side. One piece will not be enough to satisfy your craving for specialty pizza.

Poor Gary's Pizza
401 Elm Ave., Moose Lake, 218-485-8020

Log Cabin Pizza
513 Main St. S, Browerville, 320-461-0101

Happy Joe's Pizza and Ice Cream
705 E Robert St., Crookston, 218-281-5141
1700 N Broadway, New Ulm, 507-359-9811
happyjoes.com

MUSIC
AND ENTERTAINMENT

STROLL THROUGH
THE COMO PARK CONSERVATORY

In addition to lots of trees, flowers, and gardens, the conservatory has great architectural displays. Rocks, trees, and plants are used for design and function. The Japanese garden is breathtaking in summer when the water lilies are in bloom. It has received several awards and is visited by people from across the oceans. The collection of perfectly maintained bonsai trees fills me with a sense of peace and wonder. How do the gardeners trim each plant with such symmetry?

Inside the Marjorie McNeely Conservatory, color blooms despite the cold and snow outside. It's a lovely break from winter, especially for folks with seasonal depression. Each season brings different events including flower shows, master gardener discussions, bonsai care discussions, and weddings, lots of weddings. I know two people who were married at the Como Park Conservatory and they loved the venue. They joke about not needing bouquets of flowers because they were surrounded by live plants. Visitors are encouraged to visit often to view the flora and fauna changes.

1225 Estabrook Dr., St. Paul, 651-487-8201
comozooconservatory.org

VIEW A MOVIE
AT THE LONG DRIVE-IN THEATER

The Long Drive-In Theater is a summer treasure in the little town of Long Prairie. People drive for miles to grab a cold soda, buttered popcorn, and classic hot dog before they stretch out to view a lineup of new releases and summer favorites. Since 1956, moviegoers have enjoyed the big screen, great service, and nostalgic atmosphere. It's a hit with families and couples of all ages. People often bring their pet dogs to watch the show, too. Nothing beats a scary movie, or a tearjerker with your faithful pooch!

The parking area can hold over 300 cars, so there is plenty of space for your SUV. Minnesota was once home to hundreds of drive-in theaters, but only six remain. A neat summer road trip idea is to see how many you can visit from May until they close in late summer.

24257 Riverside Dr., Long Prairie, 320-732-3142
thelongdrivein.com

WALK THE WORLD'S LARGEST CORN MAZE
AT STONEY BROOK FARMS, INC.

The largest corn maze in the world is located just outside of Foley, near Saint Cloud. The 2022 giant 110-acre corn maze has 32 miles of pathways designed to look like classic Halloween villains. Will you get lost shuffling through Chucky or Pennywise? No worries, there are plenty of ways out and the entire maze is surrounded by a walking path, which will lead folks back to the entrance. The maze is appropriate for families and adventuresome adults.

Brad Chmielewski and his family love Halloween, the farm, and sharing it with folks from the weekend after Labor Day through the last weekend in October. In addition to the corn maze, Harvest Fun Days includes a corn pit, pumpkin patch, face painting, a pumpkin slingshot, pumpkin bowling, and other fall favorites. It's a wonderful way to spend a beautiful fall weekend. Bring your camera and preferably cash for your admission fee and purchases of farm-fresh foods. Three food trucks will refuel visitors if they need some extra energy to tackle Freddy Krueger's large nose.

989 115th Ave. NE, Foley, 320-333-7736
stoneybrookfarms.com

TIP

Sunflower mazes are gaining popularity! Try the Gibbon Sunflower Field for a modern take on a family favorite.

ENJOY MULTIPLE CONCERTS
WITH THE LAKES AREA MUSIC FESTIVAL

For over a decade, Central Minnesota is the place to be in July and August for the Lakes Area Music Festival. Each summer, a well-planned theme is chosen to highlight both voices and instruments as they combine to perform opera, orchestra, and chamber music. Concerts and community outreach events are held throughout the area including in the new Gichi-ziibi Center for the Arts in Brainerd High School. Gichi-ziibi is Ojibwe and translates into "a big river," the Mississippi River. The name is very fitting: the Mighty Mississippi is only a few blocks from the performance hall.

The 2022 concert season began with a summer solstice celebration/annual fundraiser featuring raffles, auctions, fine food, and of course, music. Proceeds earned were used to bring professional musicians into local schools. A Concert for Kids in late July wrapped up a weeklong day camp where kids really got into the action. Family concerts, adult fundraisers, and abundant fellowship abounded. Concerts and events are listed on the Lakes Area Music Festival website.

218-831-0765
lakesareamusic.org

ENJOY A GREAT MUSICAL
AT THE ORDWAY

Love big Broadway shows, but can't travel to New York? The Ordway Center for Performing Arts holds your ticket to award-winning entertainment. Performances include vocal artists, music, dance, and of course, Broadway musical theater. Attending a Broadway musical at the Ordway is a magical experience. Picture yourself in an opulent theater with spacious seating, intricate detailing, and your favorite person in the seat next to you.

The lights dim and a "hush" takes over the audience. It's so quiet you can hear a feather drop. Your eyes are glued to a motionless stage. Suddenly, there is tremendous action. An organ blasts out the *Phantom of the Opera Overture*, and a gold chandelier drops from the ceiling, crashing to the floor before you. Your senses are inundated with lights, music, and voices. For hours, you are drawn into the story. The final note vanishes in the night, and the spell is broken. You leave speechless, hungry for more.

345 Washington St., St. Paul, 651-224-4222
ordway.org

CATCH MUSIC AND MORE
AT A COUNTY FAIR

Minnesotans love the Minnesota State Fair, and rightfully so. It's one of the largest and best state fairs in the USA! But why wait until late August to enjoy awesome bands, 4-H booths, exciting rides, friendly competition, and fair food? All summer long, folks can enjoy affordable, fun, and local entertainment at county fairs. In a typical year, there are 90 county fairs; 40 are held in August alone!

The oldest and longest running in its current location is the Blue Earth County Fair, which has been running for over 150 years in Garden City. The Blue Earth County Fair is typically held the last weekend of July.

The largest county fair is the Steele County Free Fair, held in mid-August in Owatonna. Hundreds of thousands of visitors enjoy five stages of entertainment. The White Sidewalls, Johnny Holm Band, Wendinger Band (a polka favorite), Mason Dixon Line, and tribute bands such as Arch Allies have performed during this six-day event.

Blue Earth County Fair
335 Fairgrounds St., Garden City
507-420-5689
blueearthcountyfair.org

Steele County Free Fair
1525 S Cedar Ave., Owatonna
507-451-5305
scff.org

For a complete list of Minnesota County Fairs, visit countyfairgrounds.net

TIP

County "Best of Show" awards often lead to the opportunity to participate in the Great Minnesota Get-Together. When at a county fair, pay attention to the ribbon winners, and then follow their progress at the Minnesota State Fair.

SEE
THE GIANT ARDENT MILLS GRAIN SILO ART

In an effort to become the "artiest town in Southern Minnesota," a monumental project began in 2018 when international artist Guido van Helten was commissioned to complete a mural on the Ardent Mills Silo. The 135-foot-tall artwork tells the story of Greater Mankato including both Native and non-Native community representation. The four-sided mural represents the rich diversity and culture of the area from its earliest days. By walking the city streets and Mankato countryside, Van Helten gained an understanding of the community.

Viewing the large mural cannot be done from standing on one side. I found walking on both the River Walk and North Riverfront Drive gave me the full view. The murals cover all eight silos; each side depicts a different scene that represents Mankato area culture, past and present. The silo side facing the River Walk consists of a group of teenagers hanging out together, one in traditional powwow regalia. I highly recommend Greater Mankato visitors take the time to view this massive masterpiece.

Ardent Mills Mankato Mill
324 N Riverfront Dr., Mankato, 507-388-1062
cityartmankato.com/tours/silo-art

TIP

After viewing the Ardent Mills
Silo Art, take a walking tour of the
Mankato Sculpture Walk.

TOUR
THE MINNESOTA MUSIC HALL OF FAME

The Minnesota Music Hall of Fame celebrates music from across all genres. Located in the old library (I loved reading there as a child) exhibits large and small celebrate the influence of music in Minnesota history. The Six Fat Dutchmen and Schell's Hobo Band are just around the corner from Prince, John Denver, and the Andrews Sisters.

Folk singer-songwriter Bob Dylan and R & B singer-songwriter Prince are two of Minnesota's most recognized musicians in the building. Other popular exhibits include Judy Garland, who is most well known for her role as Dorothy in the 1939 movie *The Wizard of Oz* and in the original *A Star Is Born*. Each display has an information sheet highlighting the musicians' early life and career highlights. There is also an extensive audio tour that guides visitors from start to finish. With over 350 inductees, you'll want to give yourself hours to fully appreciate our Minnesota Music Hall of Fame.

27 Broadway St. N, New Ulm, 507-354-7305
mnmusichalloffame.org

TIP

The Minnesota Music Hall of Fame is close to downtown New Ulm, where you can experience great German food and some of the area's most famous beverages. Enjoy the traditional German architecture and historical signs.

EXPERIENCE TALENT
AT PENUMBRA THEATRE

The Penumbra Theatre has been called a snug and bright performing arts theater. My experience there was so much more. As with theaters of this caliber, the goal of high-quality entertainment is achieved. Lights, sound, stage setting, and believable characters bring the audience into the story.

Actors also challenged and encouraged audience members to view their performance through the lens of equity. Knowledge is key to healing racial wounds. I was entertained and challenged to experience learning in a new way. Study guides, workshop dates, and equity trainings are offered and found on the Penumbra Theatre's website for continued conversation. For over 40 years, this Minnesota treasure has been working within its walls to encourage equity, wellness, and difficult conversations in order to heal.

Black Nativity, *Sugar in Our Wounds*, and *What I Learned in Paris* are a handful of upcoming performances. Penumbra Theatre's website is easy to navigate and has a wealth of information on it.

270 N Kent St., St. Paul, 651-224-3180
penumbratheatre.org

APPRECIATE
MANKATO'S WALKING SCULPTURE TOUR

Historic downtown Mankato hardly resembles its footprint from the 1990s. The city center core has evolved to reflect the growing art scene and the community's desire to be the "artiest town" in southern Minnesota. Just a few blocks from the giant grain silo murals begins a sculpture walk that includes about 30 sculptures. The number varies from year to year and begins anew each spring.

Artists enter their designs into a juried pool. Each May, an Artist Dinner and Installation Day mark a new year of sculptures. Sculptures are made of steel, bronze, stained glass, lead, and a variety of other materials. Each piece reflects the artists' vision.

I admired *All the World* while attending a conference in 2021. The bronze sculpture captured a little girl dressed in a peacoat and holding an old-fashioned suitcase. The girl gazed up at a directional sign. It reminded me of the book *The Lion, the Witch, and the Wardrobe*.

CityArt Mankato Sculpture Tour
3 Civic Center Plaza, Mankato, 507-388-1062
cityartmankato.com

LISTEN TO
SEMIPROFESSIONAL CHORALE MUSIC

Semiprofessional chorale groups foster a love of music and performance for adults and children across the state. Most groups hold yearly auditions and have regular practices leading up to performances. Some groups perform only two or three concerts a year; other groups perform at monthly concerts and community events. Whether you sing in the chorus or tap your toes in the audience, the thrill of choir music lives on.

The Concord Singers were established in 1931 and are known for singing festive German music. The chorus preserves the strong musical heritage of New Ulm. Their traditional German attire makes them easy to identify at events.

Greater Minnesota is home to the Legacy Chorale, an adult choir that draws singers from multiple communities. Singers have the option of performing for fall, spring, or both concert seasons. New in 2022 was the Legacy Youth Chorale, an audition choir for grades three through five. The Legacy Chorale sings a wide range of music, including classical and contemporary.

The Concord Singers
507-354-8850
concordsingers.com

The Legacy Chorale
1001 Kingwood St., Ste. 114, Brainerd, 218-410-3030
legacychorale.org

STAND BY A GIANT DIORAMA
AT THE BELL MUSEUM

Minnesota's official natural history museum, the Bell Museum, is over 150 years old. Visitors can experience the planetarium special events, a Touch and See Lab, Curiosity Shop, and show-stopping nature dioramas. Although wildlife dioramas are part of the Minnesota Journey gallery's permanent exhibits, the dioramas themselves change. Current dioramas travel through Minnesota's last Ice Age, the Pleistocene epoch, to the Web of Life, which highlights our forests, prairies, woods, wetlands, and rivers, to the Imagine the Future exhibit, which looks at the large influence humans have had on the world as a whole.

The dioramas are huge, life-sized depictions of natural habitats, plants, and animals set in actual places. Viewers can imagine themselves in the picture, interacting with the scenery. In 2019, a popular diorama included a giant woolly mammoth! At this time, Elk at Inspiration Point is a must-see. The bellowing elk's pose was perfectly captured overlooking this famous Minnesota landmark. Exhibits change often, so make the Bell Museum a yearly excursion.

2088 Larpenteur Ave. W, St. Paul, 612-626-9660
bellmuseum.umn.edu

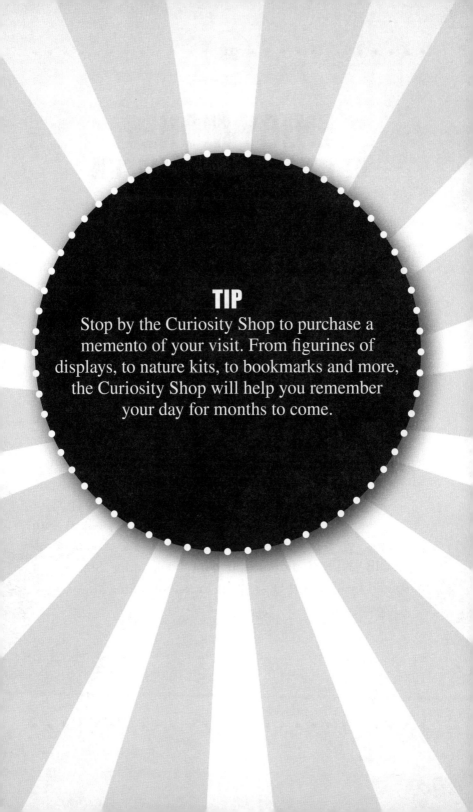

TIP

Stop by the Curiosity Shop to purchase a memento of your visit. From figurines of displays, to nature kits, to bookmarks and more, the Curiosity Shop will help you remember your day for months to come.

ENJOY MONET
AT THE MINNESOTA MARINE ART MUSEUM

The Minnesota Marine Art Museum helps visitors explore our past and ongoing relationship with water through visual art. The museum is located on the shores of the Mississippi River in Winona and features six galleries of world-class art, educational and event space, a retail shop, live art demonstrations, musical performances, and more!

Since 2006, the Minnesota Marine Art Museum has educated visitors about the importance of water through art. On my last visit, I viewed several Monet paintings; *Washington Crossing the Delaware*; Maria Svarbova: Swimming Pool; and many additional water-related paintings, ceramics, and sculptures. Maria's collection was simple yet thought provoking.

Each gallery is accessible; benches allow visitors to ponder the art and the artist. The retail store was well stocked with postcards, greeting cards, books, and art kits. My children especially enjoyed the collection of bookmarks. Small-town hospitality with world-class art on the shores of the Mississippi.

800 Riverview Dr., Winona, 507-474-6626
mmam.org

BE ENTERTAINED
IN HASTINGS

The beautiful St. Croix River runs through Hastings and provides a natural backdrop for entertainment. Wild Aventures provides guided boat trips for up to six adults. Bring your favorite camera because beaver, otter, waterfowl, and other wildlife are just around the river bend. Maybe your idea of entertainment is catching fish; the guides will lead you to the best fishing holes in town. If you're a romantic, the river is a unique setting to say, "I do!"

Live out your childhood dream of driving a real bulldozer at Extreme Sandbox. Ten acres of prime sand and dirt provide hours of digging fun. Grab your hard hat and a bunch of friends, crush a car, drive a real fire truck, or run some of your favorite heavy construction equipment. Safety first, fun always. Call ahead to reserve your afternoon.

Wild Adventures, Hastings
612-242-0554
wildadventuresmn.com

Extreme Sandbox
1901 Glendale Rd., Hastings, 855-344-4386
extremesandbox.com

Safari North Wildlife Park (page 56)

SPORTS
AND RECREATION

INTERACT WITH WILD ANIMALS
AT SAFARI NORTH WILDLIFE PARK

Kids and adults alike enjoy interacting with wildlife from around the globe at Safari North Wildlife Park. Take a ride on the Safari Express where zebra and camels walk next to the train. When you're done, feed carrots to Jigsaw or Puzzles, the giraffes. Camel rides, a petting zoo, gemstone mining, a snack shack, a large gift shop, and over 100 exhibits make this one of the largest wildlife parks in Minnesota.

Each year, new exhibits are created and current exhibits are updated. In 2022, a new black bear enclosure was created with a waterfall and pond for the bears to enjoy. Also new in 2022, Safari Scare! Open Friday and Saturday evenings in October, a great end to the Safari North season. Changes to the park occur almost monthly, so a season pass is a good idea.

8493 State Hwy. 371, Brainerd, 218-454-1662
safarinorth.com

WANDER THROUGH
THE LIVING LEGACY GARDENS

The Living Legacy Gardens is a perfect roadside detour on long trips. Founded in 2000, the gardens are tucked away near Central Lakes College. The main gardens are sun loving and include trees, bushes, annuals, and perennials. The rosebushes are delightful in July and August! Their color lights the evening sunsets.

Every plant in the Living Legacy Gardens is Zone 3 hearty, so they can handle the harsh winters of the area. Exploring the gardens each season is recommended because something new is always blooming. There are shade gardens with dozens of hostas, bleeding hearts, and ferns. The 10-acre gardens include a children's garden, butterfly enclosure, and pollinator garden buzzing with excitement. Even the tiny fairy garden is enchanting.

Volunteers and well-marked signs inform visitors of the plants' names. There are seasonal events listed on their website.

26505 County Rd. 2, Staples, 218-296-2795
clcagandenergy.org

LIGHT UP YOUR EVENING
AT WOW! ZONE

How do you recreate? Laser tag? Bowling? Arcade games? Maybe mini golfing in the dark?

Wow! Zone in Mankato has it all.

Laser tag is great fun and takes a bit of skill. Ducking between walls and sneaking up the second-floor staircase in low light is energizing. When you need a change of pace, a friendly round of mini golf is in order. This black light course is a challenge.

The 24-lane bowling alley includes a beverage and snack bar. Playing games makes people very hungry. Good thing Wow! Zone houses a sports bar and a full-service restaurant. Don't eat too much though; the arcade awaits. From carnival favorites to Duck Hunt, the Wow! Zone has dozens of games. It's all flashing lights, beeps, dings, and whistles until tickets fly from the game and you're on your way to collect your prizes. Children and adults enjoy hours of fun at Wow! Zone.

2030 Adams St., Mankato, 507-625-2695
wowzonefec.com

FLY A KITE YEAR-ROUND
AT LAKE HARRIET

Go ahead, fly a kite. In fact, fly a kite in January on Lake Harriet with thousands of other people. The sky blazes every mid-January with kites of all sizes, colors, and shapes. From classic diamond-shaped kites in just one color to ornate rainbow-colored, animal-shaped kites several feet long, Lake Harriet's Winter Kite Festival is a top "Thing" to do in Minnesota before you die. Most people fly kites in spring or summer, but this festival has been around for over 20 years, encouraging people to get out and enjoy winter.

If flying a kite in winter doesn't sound ideal to you, you could give dogsledding, ice fishing, fat tire biking, or snowshoeing a try. Maybe outdoor winter weather isn't your thing; try to fly kites in the other three seasons at Lake Harriet. While wandering the park, spot the elf house at the base of the elusive ash tree. Local legends say that anyone who leaves a letter for the elf will find a reply within three days. Even elves need a pen pal.

4135 Lake Harriet Pkwy., Minneapolis
lindenhills.org/kite-festival

SEE BISON
AT MINNEOPA STATE PARK

Bison once roamed Minnesota freely. By the early 1800s, they were no longer found in our prairies and grasslands. Thanks to a partnership between the Minnesota Department of Natural Resources and the Minnesota Zoo, 130 bison now roam between three locations: Minneopa State Park, Blue Mound State Park, and the Minnesota Zoo. There are more than 20 bison living on the Minneopa range; the lone bull is from Roosevelt National Park in North Dakota.

The fenced-in bison range is 331 acres. Visitors are advised to stay on the outside of all fencing. Maintaining at least 75 feet from the animals and avoiding loud noises and sudden movements is advised.

The best viewing area for me was Seppmann Mill lookout above the range. The bison are large, stately animals and have individual personalities. With multiple visits to the park, you may learn to identify each bison. In addition to bison watching, Minneopa has two waterfalls, an 1864 stone mill structure, hiking trails, and great wildlife viewing.

54497 Gadwall Rd., Mankato, 507-386-3910
dnr.state.mn.us/state_parks/park.html?id=spk00235#homepage

TIP

A state park sticker is required to enter the park. The sticker can be used at any of Minnesota's 60-plus state parks.

ASPIRE TO RELAX
AT INSPIRATION PEAK

Sinclair Lewis, the first US author to receive a Nobel Prize in Literature, chided all Minnesotans in the early 1930s for not experiencing Inspiration Peak. It was a sight to behold for the author, one that brought him much pleasure. After visiting Inspiration Peak myself, I concur with Mr. Lewis. The view from this standpoint is truly something to behold.

From the summit at just over 1,700 feet, over 50 lakes can be viewed in a 20-mile circle. The peak towers 400 feet over the surrounding area, giving excellent viewing of seasonal changes to Otter Tail County and to the hills in the distance. In spring and summer, tall prairie grasses sway in the gentle breezes. Three seasons of wildflowers color the quarter-mile, steep trail that climbs to the peak. If you choose to visit this Minnesota Wayside Park just once, do so in the fall. The oak, maple, and birch leaves will color the countryside with a palate of color worthy of several photographs.

Leaf Mountain Township
ottertailcountymn.us/building/inspiration-peak

TIP
Minnesota Wayside Park is a prime location for graduation and engagement photographs.

FISH
THE NORTHWEST ANGLE

The northernmost tip of Minnesota is also the northernmost part of the contiguous United States. The most unusual fact about this stretch of land is that it does not touch any part of Minnesota. To reach the Northwest Angle, visitors must cross into Canada and travel south to Minnesota. Surrounded by Lake of the Woods and Manitoba, the Northwest Angle is called a partial exclave: a piece of land that can only be entered by entering another country.

Commonly referred to as just "Angle," this small land mass is surrounded by fish. Huge fish including lake sturgeon, northern pike, and muskellunge (muskie). In May 2020, a black sturgeon weighing over 200 pounds was recorded. Big fish take patience to reel in and the right tackle. Fishermen and women will want to make sure they understand the fishing and travel regulations for both the US and Canada as they travel between the two countries. The lure of big fish is calling; will you follow?

lakeofthewoodsmn.com/northwest-angle
ezbordercrossing.com

TIP

This adventure will take careful planning. To cross the border, you will need a passport, pass card, or enhanced driver's license. Fishing licenses should be purchased in advance.

WADE THE MIGHTY MISSISSIPPI
AT ITASCA STATE PARK

The Mighty Mississippi begins in Itasca State Park and winds its way 2,500 miles to the Gulf of Mexico. At its source, the river moves so slowly that adults can wade across the boulder-strewn headwaters. But take care: the rocks beneath the surface are covered with algae and can be slippery. The water you wade across here takes three months to reach the gulf. This is also the cleanest section of the Mississippi so wading is delightful and the cool water feels great on hiking-tired feet in late summer.

Itasca State Park is Minnesota's oldest state park, and one of the largest, spanning over 32,000 acres. Overnight camping is available, but sites fill up well before summer begins. A state park sticker is required to access the park by motorized vehicle. The sticker can be used at all 66 state parks, so you can tour a different park every weekend!

36750 Main Park Dr., Park Rapids, 218-699-7251
dnr.state.mn.us/state_parks/park.html?id=spk00181#homepage

TIP

Itasca State Park bursts with color each fall. If you plan to wade in the Mississippi River, water shoes are recommended as is a hiking stick.

SEE
THE NORTHERN LIGHTS

Social media outlets and science geeks love trying to predict when the aurora borealis (northern lights) are going to make an appearance. Aurora hunters chart the probability of seeing ribbons of blue, green, and violet colors stream from the sky. Where and when is the best place to see this natural phenomenon? March is usually the best month; however, in 2022, summer sightings of the aurora borealis were spectacular.

The "where" depends a lot on the sun and how hard it pulls on Earth's magnetic field. Electrons travel to Earth and collide with nitrogen and oxygen molecules, making them go wild. When electrons calm down, they release light, which is part of the color we see, and on a rare occasion hear as a whizzing, crackling, or buzzing noise.

The best viewing of the northern lights occurs in the northern quarter of Minnesota, away from city lights. Cook County is a prime viewing area with Lutsen, Grand Marais, Grand Portage, and the Gun Flint Trail being great spots to view the lights.

Use the following website to assist you in planning your trip:
swpc.noaa.gov

RECREATE
ON LAKE SUPERIOR

Lake Superior is the world's largest freshwater lake. Its surface area is over 31,000 miles. Despite cold water temperatures, Lake Superior is a great place to recreate all year. From ice fishing in winter to wading and picking agates in summer, Minnesotans love their Lake Superior. Canoeing, kayaking, jet skiing, and swimming often entail a wet suit and life jacket. Riptides are present during stormy weather. Pay close attention to weather warnings before recreating on the big lake.

A favorite pastime is hiking from Jay Cook State Park to just before the US-Canada border on the Superior Hiking Trail. The trail is 310 miles long and weaves through the Sawtooth Mountains, past waterfalls, deep forests, and seven state parks. There are 90 backpacking sites along the northern part of the trail. Listed as one of the most scenic hiking trails in America, this trail is a challenge for novice hikers. Novice hikers are encouraged to hike sections of the trail with other hikers.

Superior Hiking Trail
superiorhiking.org
lakesuperiorstreams.org

SWIM
AT FLANDRAU STATE PARK

Minnesota has 66 state parks, each known for a different characteristic. Flandrau State Park near New Ulm has one of the best swimming beaches in the area. The sandy bottom feels great on sunburned feet and provides better footing for new swimmers. The swimming pond is open from early June until the third weekend of August and has a lifeguard on staff during busier times on weekends. Parents are encouraged to watch their children at all times.

In addition to a great swimming pond, Flandrau offers camper cabins, which can be reserved in advance; campsites for RV and tent camping; and historic buildings from the 1930s, including some used while the park was a World War II German prisoner-of-war camp. WPA and CCC projects have signage to help visitors understand the importance of building projects of this era. New Ulm is just a few miles away and offers grocery stores, shopping, Schell's Brewery and Gardens, historic sites, and other amenities.

1300 Summit Ave., New Ulm, 507-233-1260
dnr.state.mn.us/state_parks/park.html?id=spk00145#homepage

TAKE THE KIDS
TO CROSBY MEMORIAL PARK

Crosby Memorial Park overlooks Serpent Lake and provides three seasons of entertainment. The campground offers 20 RV sites and six additional tent sites. Families can enjoy Crosby's small-town atmosphere with a large, modern playground, picnic shelter, and band shelter. Serpent Lake offers good fishing and room for water sports. Moms and dads can take turns relaxing under the giant sea serpent that protects the shoreline. He's a great prop for family photos.

If the kids need to burn off energy, the Cuyuna Lakes Mountain Bike Trails are a short distance away. Remember to wear old shoes and dark clothing: the iron-rich soil will stain white shoes and light-colored clothing. If you need to cool down and relax for a bit, stop by Victual (#3) for some of the best ice cream in Minnesota. Lemon and other fruit flavors are perfect on hot days.

2 2nd St. SW, Crosby, 218-546-5021
cityofcrosby.com

PLAY PICKLEBALL
AT RIVER'S EDGE PARK

Is this a sport thing or entertainment? I guess it depends on who is playing, and how long you've known the players. If I'm playing, it is definitely entertainment. But for many people, it's a competitive sport. What is pickleball? It is a newer sport that combines three favorite summer sports: tennis, table tennis, and badminton. Like tennis, it is played on a court with a net. The pickleball court is smaller than in tennis, so there is less running. The rules are simple and the paddles are bigger than those used in table tennis.

River's Edge Park offers six pickleball courts that are free to play on. The courts open at 8 a.m. and close around 8 p.m. You just need to show up with your equipment to play. The park also offers a splash pad, plenty of green space to roam on, a playground, disc golf, picnic areas, and more. During the winter, the outdoor pickleball courts are closed; indoor courts may be found at many YMCAs and resorts.

1300 Great Oak Dr., Waite Park, 320-252-6955
ci.waitepark.mn.us/facilities/facility/details/riversedgepark-6

TIP

Looking for other courts in Minnesota?
pickleball-near-me.com and places2play.org
can help you find a course near you.

PONDER
THE JEFFERS PETROGLYPHS

In Southern Minnesota's Prairie land lies thousands of sacred rock carvings called petroglyphs. The carvings predate Native Americans and tell the stories of their early ancestors. Images of prairie animals such as bison, beaver, and turtles can be found as well as Thunderbirds and other Native American symbols. The Jeffers Petroglyphs are made of Sioux quartzite outcroppings and are part of the Minnesota Historical Society. Visitors may take the designated path and explore the petroglyphs at their own pace, or take a guided tour. Visitors are reminded that this site is considered sacred; it is one of the oldest continuously used sacred sites in the world.

Staff are on the path and can help visitors understand what the carvings are and their significance. Additional carvings were recently discovered covered with lichen; they are being carefully preserved. The rock face is open June 1 until mid-September on Thursday, Friday, and Saturday evenings.

27160 County Rd. 2, Comfrey, 507-628-5591
mnhs.org/jefferspetroglyphs

TIP

The uneven surfaces can make navigating the rock surface difficult. Walking barefoot or stocking footed is sometimes safer. Bring a hiking stick and water bottle.

GOLF
AT CRAGUN'S LEGACY COURSES

The Tom Lehman Signature Golf Course at Cragun's Legacy Courses is open and offers some of the best golfing in the state, perhaps some of the best in the Midwest. Major renovations have created 54 holes of PGA-quality golf. Lehman is a PGA Tour professional and the designer of the latest renovations. This project is something to behold. The course has been expanded and highlights not only the beauty of Cragun's Northwoods property, but also the sport of golf. From a beginner par 3 course to the "Lehman 18" and "Dutch 27," golfers of all levels will be challenged and have the opportunity to enjoy a day in the sun.

Lakeside cabins, lakeside hotel rooms, and other on-site lodging options keep you close to the course and family. Beautiful Gull Lake is just outside your window and will call you back year after year. Golf and vacation packages are available.

11000 Craguns Dr., Brainerd, 866-988-0562
craguns.com

CHILL BY
THE DETROIT LAKES ICE PALACE

February is the perfect month to put on your mukluks and walk a few laps around the Detroit Lakes Pavilion. Bring the whole family to acknowledge the region's ice harvesting history. The worst of winter is on its way out in February, and the days are getting longer. Cabin fever is upon us.

A trip to the Ice Palace draws us to the beauty of winter and gets us some vitamin D. The palace is over 30 feet high and 95 feet wide. The ice blocks glow a mystical blue in the light of dusk. King Isbit's throne stands before the palace, ready for your family photo. Professionally carved sculptures, a lit children's maze, ice golf, and outdoor music add to the fun. Bundle up and chill in Detroit Lakes.

1362 Washington Ave., Detroit Lakes
iceharvestdl.org

DESCEND THE SOUDAN MINE
AT LAKE VERMILION-SOUDAN UNDERGROUND STATE PARK

Minnesota is a mining state, producing 40 million tons of iron ore each year. Minnesota's oldest and deepest iron ore mine is no longer active, making it the perfect place to explore! From 1884 until 1962, the Soudan Mine grew deeper and deeper until it reached a depth of 2,341 feet. The 27-level tour takes about 1.5 hours and is available from Memorial Day weekend through Labor Day for ages five and up. Don your hard hat (provided), jacket, and walking shoes for a bumpy ride to the depths of a real iron ore mine.

The state park is open 12 months a year and has much to experience in addition to the mine tours. Eight camper cabins are available for park users to rent, which makes it easy to enjoy day after day of hiking, biking, animal watching, and simple communing with nature. Rent a cabin in fall to get a great burst of colors!

Summer: 1302 McKinley Park Rd., Soudan
October through May: 1379 Stuntz Bay Rd., Soudan
218-300-7000
dnr.state.mn.us/state_parks/park.html?id=spk00285#homepage

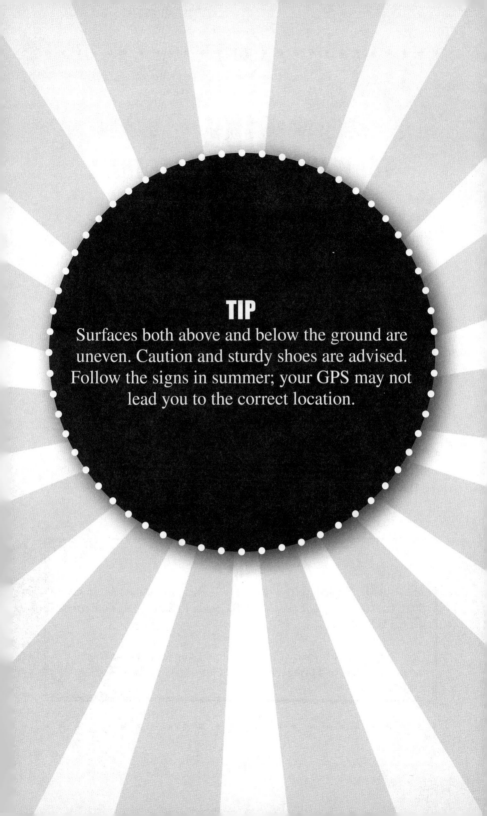

TIP

Surfaces both above and below the ground are uneven. Caution and sturdy shoes are advised. Follow the signs in summer; your GPS may not lead you to the correct location.

BIKE
THE PAUL BUNYAN STATE TRAIL

The Paul Bunyan State Trail covers 120 miles, from Crow Wing State Park north to Bemidji. The paved trail is handicap accessible and perfect for all-season recreation including hiking, in-line skating, snowshoeing, walking, geocaching, and all kinds of biking. Small children enjoy the flat surface when riding bikes with training wheels. Adult-sized mountain bikes and fat-tire bikes are great for the longer journeys. New to the trail, electric bicycles are making traveling the entire 120 miles in a summer easier than ever.

The trail weaves through 14 Northwoods communities and has rest stops along the way. Maps are available at area businesses or on the website below.

paulbunyantrail.com

TIP

The Paul M. Thiede Fire Tower Park is located just off the Paul Bunyan State Trail near Pequot Lakes at 5230 County Road 10. The view from the top is amazing!

Don't forget to refill your water bottle if you stop for a snack. Wear a helmet for safety and bring a first aid kit for those little mishaps.

Paul M. Tiede Fire Tower Park
just off the Paul Bunyan Trail (page 63)

Grab Barbecue at Wilbur's on Walker Bay (page 6)

WALKER

WI

on

SPOR

WILBURSONWALI

MINNESOTA

BUR'S

Walker Bay

BAR & EATERY

RBAY.COM

Recreate on Lake Superior (page 69)

See Bison at Minneopa State Park (page 60)

Travel North to the Amethyst Mine Panorama (page 154)

Wander through the Living Legacy Gardens (page 57)

Chill by the Detroit Lakes Ice Palace (page 77)

Indulge in German Culture at Domeier's (page 108)

Interact with Wild Animals at Safari North Wildlife Park (page 56)

Wade the Mighty Mississippi at Itasca State Park (page 66)

Walk the World's Largest Corn Maze at Stoney Brook Farms, Inc. (page 38)

Admire Ken Nyberg Sculptures (page 97)

ADMIRE
KEN NYBERG SCULPTURES

A life-size replica of NASA astronaut Karen Nyberg sits in the Nyberg Sculpture Garden near a giant elephant in Nyberg Park. The park is named after the astronaut's father, Ken Nyberg. Nyberg has created over 50 metal sculptures since the 1980s. His earliest creations were formed with scrap metal as Nyberg perfected his skills.

Once Nyberg retired, the sky became his limit and his hobby became his life's passion. Many of his sculptures are located in Nyberg Park next to Big Foot Gas & Grocery. The gas station is not named after the hairy creature, but rather one of Nyberg's earlier sculptures: an unusually large foot with a giant big toe. Other sculptures within the park include a 14-foot pliers with a huge roach near the top, an eight-foot-tall square knot, and a 12-foot-tall knife and spoon. Nyberg has many more outside his shop near Vining. Please visit his website for exact locations of his sculptures; he is hard at work on several more!

6001 E Front St., Vining, 218-769-4484
nybergsculptures.com

TIP
Grab a slice of hot pizza and a cold soda at Big Foot Gas & Grocery before viewing the sculptures. The park has several picnic tables to sit at. The sculptures make a great backdrop for humorous photos of the kids.

VISIT HALLOCK,
HOME OF MINNESOTA'S FIRST INDOOR HOCKEY ARENA

Never heard of Hallock? I see a road trip in your future. Hallock offers tons of recreational activities, including world-class bird-watching, camping, golfing, snowshoeing, cross-country skiing, and snowmobiling. The sport this town of 906 is really known for is hockey. In 1894, Hallock had the first indoor Minnesota hockey arena. In 1895, it was torn down and a new arena was built. That year, the first recorded hockey game was played in Hallock. A few years later, in 1906, the arena collapsed. Since 1974, the current rink has been serving the skaters of Hallock and the surrounding area.

It is interesting to note that Hallock is in the Red River Valley, one of the most fertile lands in Minnesota. Located just 20 miles from the Canada-US border, this town is definitely in the north country. All summer, farmers farm their fields and grow some of the nation's most prized crops. All winter, these same families enjoy the sport of hockey!

163 3rd St. N, Hallock, 218-843-2626
hallockyouthhockey.com

TIP

Need to warm up after a game? Far North
Spirits is the furthermost distillery in the
continental US. It is one of the few distilleries
that prides itself in making whiskey that goes
from field to glass in one town.

farnorthspirits.com

KICK BACK
AT CHASE ON THE LAKE

The original 1922 Chase Hotel was a grand, luxurious building that was destined from the start to be one of Minnesota's most popular summer hotels. The rise of the resort industry provided the area with an influx of tourists year-round. From summer vacationers to winter weather enthusiasts, Chase Hotel served hundreds of people with northern hospitality. The early hotel had a restaurant and a saloon. In 1997, a kitchen fire caused extensive damage to the hotel; it was razed in 2007.

In its place, a four-season luxury resort hotel rose from the ashes. A pair of leaded glass doors from the 1922 hotel was used to recreate the grand 1920s style. The current Chase on the Lake sits perpendicular to Walker Bay. Resort and conference attendees are encouraged to relax on the private beach or take a few laps in the indoor swimming pool. Chase on the Lake is just a few blocks from downtown Walker where visitors can wander through the Walker General Store (#89) or grab barbecue at Wilbur's on Walker Bay (#4).

502 Cleveland Blvd. W, Walker, 218-547-7777
chaseonthelake.com

SKI MINNESOTA

Minnesota has almost 20 alpine ski and snowboard areas spread across the state; on-site and nearby resorts offer all-season recreation. Two favorites are Eagle Ridge Resort and Wild Mountain Resort near Taylor Falls.

Eagle Ridge Resort has ski-in/ski-out access to the 40 kilometers of slopes and seven lifts of the Lutsen Mountains. It's Minnesota's largest ski area and is a great stay for all levels of skiers and snowboarders. The trail cam gives guests an up-to-the-minute view of mountain conditions before they head out for the day.

Wild Mountain near Taylor Falls has four lifts and 4.8 kilometers of slopes. The beautiful Saint Croix valley is a beautiful setting for alpine skiing. In summer, go-karts, slides, and a lazy river provide a needed distraction until snow starts to fall and snow machines are turned on.

Eagle Ridge Resort
445 Ski Hill Rd., Lutsen, 800-360-7666
eagleridgeatlutsen.com

Wild Mountain
37200 Wild Mtn. Rd., Taylor Falls, 651-465-6365
wildmountain.com

ENJOY FAMILY TIME
AT SAND LAKE RESORT

Sometimes a family needs to get away for some simple, quality relaxation time. Come to think of it, sometimes close groups of friends also need a place to rejuvenate and reconnect. The Sand Lake Resort has been serving families and groups of friends since the 1920s. It's the kind of resort that offers space to fish, swim, make s'mores, and talk around a campfire. It's close to ATV trails, bike trails, tennis courts, and pickleball courts. Free Wi-Fi, TVs, and DVD players are great extras. They have boats available for rental for the last-minute vacation. Water toys, canoes, kayaks, and two playgrounds keep everyone busy and enjoying the great outdoors.

The Sand Lake Resort is located on the small bay of Sand Lake, near Sturgeon Lake. Sand Lake is known for its abundance of panfish and bass. Ice fishing and snowmobiling are favorite winter pastimes for guests of this year-round resort. In addition to one- and two-bedroom cabins, vacation homes with laundry facilities are also available.

94154 County Hwy. 61, Sturgeon Lake, 218-485-8164
sandlakeresort.com

ZIP HIGH
WITH KERFOOT CANOPY TOUR

The Minnesota River Valley takes center stage for Minnesota's number one outdoor adventure, Kerfoot Canopy Tour near Henderson. Fourteen zip lines take adventurers progressively higher, longer, and faster, reaching 175 feet above the ground. A 170-foot suspension bridge is a real test of nerves. Don't panic; training is provided.

Visitors age 10 and up weighing between 70 and 250 pounds undergo "Ground School" to learn the ropes before starting their adventure. Kerfoot Canopy Tour also offers a High Ropes Course with 60 challenges taking visitors 50 feet above ground. The changing Minnesota Valley colors are a delight to behold from this height.

Sister company Brainerd Zip Line Tour offers seven zip lines and a suspension bridge to give zip liners a view of Pillsbury State Park from high in the air. The 2.5-hour tour gives adrenaline junkies a big thrill. Reservations are required at both locations.

Kerfoot Canopy Tours
30200 Scenic Byway Rd., Henderson, 952-873-3900
kerfootcanopytour.com

Brainerd Zipline
9898 County Rd. 77 SW, Nisswa, 218-656-1111
zipbrainerd.com

555

555

555

555

555

555

555

555

555

EXPLORE
NIAGARA CAVE

Thing #63 took visitors high above the earth's surface. Fitting that Niagara Cave takes visitors 200 feet below the surface. This family business gives guided tours of one of *USA Today*'s "Best Caves in the USA." Open May 1 until October 30, the cave stays at a constant temperature of about 48 degrees. Pack a sweatshirt or jacket before you descend 275 stairs to see the power of an active stream, waterfall, and an ancient stream.

It's a sight to behold with traditional lighting. Adventuresome folks will want to reserve a spot on the Lantern Tours. The first quarter of the tour remains the same with traditional lighting, but the rest of the tour is by lantern. Explore the passageways with more shadows, blurred edges, and a little less clarity in the corners. A favorite for romantics is the subterranean wedding chapel.

29842 County Rd. 30, Harmony, 507-866-6606
niagaracave.com

TIP
If you really enjoy caving, the
Forestville/Mystery Cave State Park
is in nearby Preston.

dnr.state.mn.us/state_parks/
park.html?id=spk00148#homepage

This Minnesota Historical Society plaque is
found at historic sites throughout Minnesota.

CULTURE
AND HISTORY

INDULGE IN GERMAN CULTURE
AT DOMEIER'S

This little treasure first opened in 1934 and has been in the same family since day one. The store is delightful in any season; if possible, stop after Thanksgiving, when the holiday decorations are on the outside of the store. This is a special shopping season called Weihnachtsmarkt. You'll think you are in the Black Forest! If you look closely, you might spot the gnome hiding in the shop window. Nutcrackers, cuckoo clocks, and beer steins fill the snow-frosted windowpanes.

Inside, rows and rows of handblown Bohemian glass ornaments dangle from the ceiling. Around every corner, more old country merchandise awaits customers. German-Austrian music quietly plays in the corner and if you listen carefully, you will hear the thick German accent from local patrons. It is easy to find gifts for everyone on your shopping list. Children's books, tasty treats, Bavarian hats and pins, and much more fill this little store. Domeier's is truly a special place, a little treasure tucked away in New Ulm.

1020 S Minnesota St., New Ulm, 507-354-4231
call ahead for store hours

RELAX
AT ELY STEAM SAUNA

Ely Steam Sauna is the oldest continuously operated sauna service in Minnesota, and one of the oldest in the US. Since 1915, it's the "hottest place" in Ely. In the early days, saunas were a miner's bath day, providing the opportunity to wash away the iron-laced soil, soothe stiff muscles, and ease sore joints. Founded in Finland, saunas in Northern Minnesota are enjoyed by Scandinavians and every other ethnic group. Generations of families have visited Ely Steam Sauna after a week in the Boundary Waters Canoe Area Wilderness for the same health benefits the miners experienced.

Steam saunas are a great way to relax, socialize, and warm up in winter. Ely Steam Sauna has public and private sauna options; booking in advance is strongly encouraged to ensure an opening. Soap, towel, and cold showers are part of the package. You only get one body; treat it to an Ely Steam Sauna date.

127 1st Ave. E, Ely, 218-365-2984
elysteamsauna.net

TIP
While in Ely, warm your feet with a pair of Steger Mukluks (#88).

FIND PEACE
AT THE PIPESTONE
NATIONAL MONUMENT

For over 3,000 years, generations of American Indians have quarried pipestone from the Pipestone National Monument land. Considered sacred, the land and revered stone that is found in it are used to create red pipestone pipes, which are thought to carry prayers to the "Great Spirit." Under layers of hard quartzite, soft layers of red pipestone are found. Digging to the pipestone layers may take days, weeks, months, or even years. It is a labor steeped in tradition. Only members of federal-recognized tribes may apply for quarry permits.

Traditional Native American artists work the pipestone into small figures, jewelry, pipes, and other items, which can be purchased at the Pipestone Indian Shrine Association, located inside the visitor's center. The mission of the center is to preserve the vanishing art of pipe-making.

The 301-acre site is surrounded by prairie wild flowers and prairie grasses that wave in the summer breezes, bringing visitors a sense of peace.

36 Reservation Ave., Pipestone, 507-825-5464
nps.gov/pipe

TIP

If visiting the Pipestone National Monument, you are only a half hour from the Rock County Historical Center (#82).

FIND BIGFOOT
IN REMER

Bigfoot is one of Minnesota's most famous, seldomly seen men. He's occasionally spotted in the Northwoods during camping trips. Remer is the self-declared "home of Bigfoot." Each July, the town celebrates Bigfoot Days, a special weekend set aside for the big guy. Hundreds of amateur and professional "squatchers" descend on the area to collect and share evidence of the elusive, hairy creature. (A "squatcher" is someone who actively searches for Bigfoot in the wilderness.)

This part of the state has great "squatching terrain," including thousands of lakes, rivers, and streams surrounded by acres and acres of deep forestland. It's the perfect setting for a Bigfoot calling contest, a town hall meeting with the Bigfoot Research Team, a 5K run, and great music that will have you howling for more.

If crowds aren't your thing, visit the Bigfoot Gas and Gifts station another time and pose with the life-size Bigfoot silhouette. You can check out the plaster Bigfoot footprints and buy your own souvenir to commemorate your trip into Bigfoot Country.

Bigfoot Days, Remer
homeofbigfoot.com

Bigfoot Gas and Gifts
4 Etna Ave., Remer, 218-566-1629
big-foot-gas-gifts.edan.io

VOYAGE TO
THE HJEMKOMST CENTER

Much of the Red River Valley was settled by hearty Scandinavians in the 1800s, so it's fitting that the Heritage Hjemkomst Interpretive Center is located in Moorhead. The Hjemkomst Center is home to two very interesting replicas. The first is the replica of the Gakstad, a Viking ship found in Norway in the 1880s. Robert Asp, a local guidance counselor, came up with the idea to build the replica. With family and community support, the Hjemkomst, meaning "homecoming," was completed in 1980, shipped to Duluth, and christened. After sailing throughout Lake Superior, the Hjemkomst took the long voyage to Oslo, Norway, before returning to its resting place in Moorhead.

The Hopperstad Stave Church is a full-sized, wood replica of a 12th-century church from Norway. The church is made from cedar, redwood, and pine; it is located on the grounds of the Hjemkomst Center. Its shape is something to behold and is not what we typically see in Minnesota.

202 1st Ave. N, Moorhead, 218-299-5515
cityofmoorhead.com

WATCH
THE DAKOTA 38+2
WOKIKSUYE MEMORIAL RIDE

The Dakota Wokiksuye Memorial Ride begins in Lower Brule, South Dakota, and ends in Mankato, at approximately 10 a.m. on December 26. The ride began in 2008 and commemorates the 38+2 Dakota who were executed on this date in 1862. Riders leave Lower Brule and often encounter wintery conditions including snow, freezing rain, and wind. Riders travel through South Dakota and southwestern Minnesota on a solemn ride until reaching the site where the US's largest mass execution was held, by order of President Lincoln.

A group of runners leaves Fort Snelling on December 25 and joins the riders at Reconciliation Park. The ride and run honor the 38 Dakota and two chiefs executed, and is part of a reconciliation between the Dakota and Mankato communities. The message they wish to share is reconciliation and healing.

Outside the Blue Earth County Library sits *Winter Warrior*, a giant limestone sculpture of a Dakota warrior, and across the street, the county's Reconciliation Memorial. Both serve to keep the memory of the 38+2 from being forgotten.

Wokiksuye 38+2 Memorial Ride
mankatomn.gov

Blue Earth County Library
100 E Main St., Mankato
507-304-4001
beclibrary.org

VISIT
MOONSTONE FARM

A stay at Moonstone Farm will remind you of a simpler time. A time when beef was grass fed, pottery was hand thrown, and quilts sat on the foot of each cottage bed. The Broodio is a one-room cabin that visitors may rent for a relaxing stay. I toured the farm and spent an afternoon by their pond. I appreciated a small taste of prairie life with alfalfa fields, grape vines, native wildflowers, and plenty of nature all around.

Audrey and Richard welcome visitors to stay in the Broodio where they will experience the best of prairie life. In early mornings, enjoy listening to birds sing and cattle low before taking a hike on trails lined with wildflowers and tall grasses. Wander through the studio where pottery, barn quilts, honey, hemp seeds, paintings, greeting cards, essential oils, and a variety of artist wares are sold. A few days and evenings on the farm will renew your senses, recharge your soul, and remind you of a simpler time.

9060 40th St. SW, Montevideo, 320-226-2873
moonstonefarm.net

ATTEND
THE DRAGON FESTIVAL

The Dragon Festival is held every mid-July at Phalen Lake in St. Paul. It is a celebration of Asian-Pacific cultures and includes many authentic events and a plethora of culturally distinct food! In addition to food trucks, guests can learn about Asian-Pacific culture through performers, merchandise vendors, children's activities, and lots of music and dancing.

One well-attended and colorful event is the dragon boat races, which originated in China. The races are competitive, and everyone is encouraged to join a team. Each boat is 40 feet long and less than four feet in width. Intricate dragon heads and tails help identify each boat. A drummer helps the paddlers maintain a steady rhythm while they race to the finish line. Dragon racing is over 2,000 years old and this team sport is experiencing a comeback. Winning is always appreciated, as is fellowship and increased physical fitness.

Phalen Park, St. Paul
dragonfestival.org

ORDER POPCORN
AT THE HISTORIC POPCORN WAGON

Children these days can experience the thrill of ordering popcorn and other snacks from the same popcorn wagon that has been serving the New Ulm area for over 100 years. The Brown County Historical Society purchased the wagon in 2002. At that time, it was in need of tender loving care. Through a combined effort by the members of the historical society, local businesses, and community members, the wagon was returned to its glory. A fresh coat of bright red paint and lots of elbow grease were just what the wagon required.

The top half of the Popcorn Wagon is mostly glass. In pleasant weather, the windows are opened, causing the entire downtown district to smell of delicious popcorn. The Brown County Historical Society uses the proceeds from popcorn sales to further its mission. To plan your visit to see the historic wagon, please check the website below.

2 N Broadway, New Ulm, 507-233-2616
browncountyhistorymn.org/popcorn-wagon-2021-calendar

PAUSE
AT THE MILLE LACS INDIAN MUSEUM AND TRADING POST

The Mille Lacs Indian Museum and Trading Post weave together the art and culture of the Mille Lacs Band of the Ojibwe. From the 2020 Jingle Dress exhibit to the informational Four Seasons Room, this Minnesota Historical Site is packed with information. Workshops, demonstrations, exhibit scavenger hunts, and children's crafts add to family interactions.

The Trading Post's rich history dates back to 1918. The pristine log building has been restored to its 1930s charm. The site's history is important as is the continuation of cultural heritage to sustain and encourage local artists to create traditional art. Renowned artists from tribes across North America proudly offer sculptures, paintings, jewelry, beadwork, baskets, moccasins, and much more. The smallest beaded leather bags to full-sized wood sculptures are all beautifully crafted.

43411 Oneida Dr., Onamia, 320-532-3632
mnhs.org/millelacs

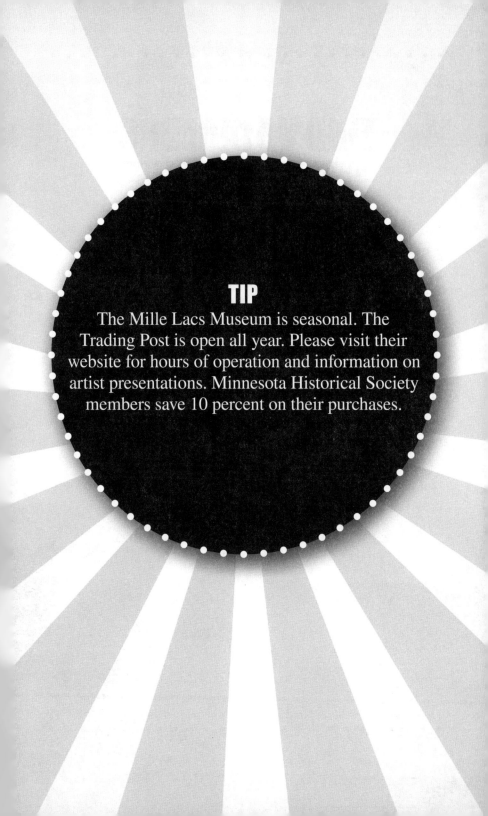

TIP

The Mille Lacs Museum is seasonal. The Trading Post is open all year. Please visit their website for hours of operation and information on artist presentations. Minnesota Historical Society members save 10 percent on their purchases.

FIND VOYAGEURS
AT THE GRAND PORTAGE
NATIONAL MONUMENT

Throughout the year, the Grand Portage National Monument gives visitors a glimpse into the rich 1800s fur trade. The National Park Service maintains the sight all year, including the Heritage Center, bookstore, archives, exhibits, and hiking trails.

Land for the monument was donated by the Grand Portage Band of the Ojibwe. Every August, Rendezvous Days is held in conjunction with the Grand Portage Ojibwe's powwow. The huge celebrations take visitors back in time through demonstrations, exhibits, music, and reenactments. Over 300 volunteers gather, many showing their talents in long-forgotten trades. Listening to the banter of the voyageurs as they go about their day is a real treat; some even converse in French! Bring your camera to preserve the history.

170 Mile Creek Rd., Grand Portage, 218-475-0123
nps.gov/grpo

TIP

Take your picnic lunch across the highway to Grand Portage State Park. The Pigeon River plunges 120 feet over a waterfall. The High Falls is quite the site in spring as it roars downstream. You will need a State Park Permit.

FOLLOW
THE JESSE JAMES GANG BANK ROBBERY

We've had our share of historic events in Minnesota. One of the most publicized occurred in 1876, when America was celebrating its 100th birthday. Northfield was already known for being home to both St. Olaf and Carleton colleges. In September of that year, another historic event occurred that put Northfield on the map for all times.

The James-Younger gang sought out banks to rob in Southern Minnesota. Their decision to rob the Northfield bank proved deadly. Citizens were alerted to the robbery, and a gunfight ensued in the streets. Two gang members and two citizens died and the largest manhunt in US history began. The Younger brothers were caught, as was another gang member. The James-Younger gang was defeated and history was made. The weekend after Labor Day, Northfield celebrates the courage of its "ordinary" citizens from 1876. A group of Northfield volunteers plans the celebration, including a reenactment of the bank robbery, parade, horseshoe hunt, and creation of a Defeat of Jesse James Day button.

djjd.org

TIP

If you miss the four-day event in August, the Northfield Historical Society occupies the First National Bank as its museum.

EXPLORE
THE MINNESOTA AFRICAN AMERICAN HERITAGE MUSEUM AND GALLERY

The Minnesota African American Heritage Museum and Gallery celebrates history, art, and the culture of Blacks in Minnesota. It is a place to view exhibitions, experience programs, further your knowledge of African American heritage, and attend community events. Their artist-in-residence program gives support and exposure to Black artists as they create new projects. The goal is to explore Black art, literature, history, and culture in Minnesota.

The MAAHMG hosts a variety of special events including "Fashion on the Rooftop," which is held in May during Black Fashion Week. Designers pull out all the stops as they create one-of-a-kind fashions. A 10-week youth curator program teaches museum curation to students ages 14–18. The participants work toward final history and art exhibitions followed by a community discussion of their experience. The students learn valuable skills and gain confidence and self-esteem.

1256 Penn Ave. N, 4th Floor, Minneapolis, 617-987-6543
maahmg.org

SEARCH FOR
BABE, PAUL, AND THE JOLLY GREEN GIANT

Minnesota's leading men can be spotted across the state. These characters include the likes of Babe the Blue Ox, Paul Bunyan, the Jolly Green Giant, Sprout, the Hamm's Bear, and Fairchild the Gopher (our Minnesota State Fair mascot), among others. Small children, and impatient adults, sometimes have difficulties on long car rides. I don't blame them; not everyone enjoys car rides as much as I do. For me, travel is about the journey, not necessarily the destination. Minnesota is about 400 miles from south to north and between 200 and 350 miles from east to west. I encourage parents to declare a scavenger hunt as they travel, and see how many statues the kids can identify.

There are leading ladies scattered across Minnesota including Lucette, Paul Bunyan's girlfriend, and Mary Tyler Moore.

Sprout and the Jolly Green Giant are found in Blue Earth.
Mary Tyler Moore is located in Minneapolis.
Paul Bunyan is in Brainerd, Akeley, Bemidji, and other communities.
Lucette is located in Hackensack.
Babe can be spotted all over the Brainerd Lakes area.

APPRECIATE
AMISH CULTURE

Just outside of Harmony, near the Iowa border, lies an old-world Amish community of over 100 families. This is Minnesota's largest Amish community. Founded in 1974, it continues to grow each year. There are multiple one-room schoolhouses, and several church districts that serve the community members. Most of the residents are farmers or carpenters. They traditionally use horse and buggy for transportation, or hire a driver, and keep to the simple ways of life. The Amish community sells their produce, jellies, jams, furniture, and quilts to local businesses. They also have roadside stands, and their own small businesses.

Amish Tours of Harmony hosts tours where visitors can learn about the Amish way of life and respectfully experience the Amish culture. Five Star Weaving is an Amish-owned shop that sells shag rugs, pot holders, and other yarn creations. The Village Green has the largest selection of Amish quilts in Minnesota.

Amish Tours of Harmony
94 2nd St. NW, Harmony, 507-886-2303
amish-tours.com

Five Star Weaving
33343 Garden Rd., Harmony

Village Green
90–94 2nd St. NW, Harmony, 507-886-2409

COUNT
BARN QUILTS

Barn Quilts of Central Minnesota built a trail of over 100 quilts through Cass, Todd, Wadena, and Morrison Counties. Barn quilts, like their fabric cousins, tell a story about the artist and their life. Each barn quilt is carefully painted on a wood board and is then attached to a barn, building, or fence post. Artists and sponsors work together to create a unique one-of-a-kind square.

The Barn Quilt Trail began when a local, talented quilter discovered barn quilts while traveling in Iowa and Missouri. Years later, her vision was realized through grants and community support. The trail has expanded to a large travel area; it takes many hours to view in one day. A smaller tour of 30-plus barn quilts begins at the Staples Historic Depot and takes about a half hour to drive. The self-guided tour map (full-color) is posted on the website below or can be found at the Historic Staples Depot.

218-894-2906
barnquiltsmn.org

SIT ON A COVERED WAGON
AT THE LAURA INGALLS WILDER MUSEUM

Life on the Minnesota prairie was an exciting adventure in the 1870s. In a series of autobiographical books, Laura Ingalls Wilder wrote about her childhood days living on the banks of Plum Creek near Walnut Grove. Her books became a hit television show that ran for nine seasons.

The Laura Ingalls Wilder Museum is a little village of eight buildings that include a depot, little red schoolhouse, chapel, and dugout (like the one Laura lived in). The buildings and historic artifacts spark visitors' curiosity into early pioneer life. Learn how people hopped up on a stagecoach, hitched up a covered wagon, and kept the sun out of their eyes while working outside. Check out the cool memorabilia donated by the show's cast.

Each September, Walnut Grove celebrates Laura Ingalls Wilder Days, giving visitors the perfect opportunity to practice their pioneer skills.

330 8th St., Walnut Grove, 507-859-2358
walnutgrove.org/museum

SEE THE WORLD'S THIRD-LARGEST NUTCRACKER COLLECTION
AT THE ROCK COUNTY HISTORICAL CENTER

The Rock County Historical Center in Luverne houses more than 4,500 nutcrackers from across the globe. Visitors from around the world enjoy the center in their new location, the former Ford dealership building. With so many nutcrackers, it's easy to see why they needed more space. Each November and December, businesses and residents get into the holiday spirit and join a huge scavenger hunt to find the names of over 120 nutcrackers. Nutcrackers are displayed throughout Luverne during the scavenger hunt.

During the rest of the year, the nutcracker collection is displayed in the historical center, in a variety of groupings including Santas, occupations, and characters. The collection is dusted and counted just once a year. Historical society members speculate that the collection now houses more nutcrackers than there are residents in Luverne (4,557 folks as of 2020). Additional nutcracker donations are added yearly by generous supporters of the center and nutcracker enthusiasts.

312 E Main St., Luverne, 507-283-2122
rockcountyhistorical.com

SEE
THE CLAYTON, JACKSON, AND MCGHIE MEMORIAL

On June 15, 1920, Elmer Jackson, Elias Clayton, and Isaac McGhie were forced from their jail cells and lynched from a light pole high above Duluth's Second Avenue East. The three young, Black circus workers were accused of raping a white woman. The accusations were unsubstantiated, but racial tensions were high, and the mob took the law into their own hands.

Although heavily publicized in the summer of 1920, by 1973, Duluth and all of Minnesota "forgot" the tragic story of the young men. Through the work of the Memorial Committee, the tragedy came into clearer focus and the memorial came to light in 2003.

The 54-by-70-foot bronze memorial does not highlight the ugliness of the lynching. Instead, artist Carla Stetson captured the three individuals as they might have been. Jackson, Clayton, and McGhie emerge from the memorial sporting their Sunday best, in relaxed stances, as though they are waiting for friends to join them and challenge viewers to create a better community.

222 E Superior St., Ste. 327, Duluth, 218-336-2990
claytonjacksonmcghie.org

WANDER THROUGH
HISTORIC WABASHA

US government records state that Wabasha was founded in 1830 and is the oldest town in Minnesota and the oldest town on the upper Mississippi River. Named after Chief Wa-pa-shaw of the Sioux Nation, this river town's historic downtown buildings are being restored to their original stature. More than 50 buildings in this town of 2,500 are listed on the National Register of Historic Places. Tour-guided or self-guided tours of the city walk visitors through historic sites and lead them to explore restaurants, small businesses, and spots for cold beverages.

The town is most known for its cameo appearance in *Grumpy Old Men* and celebrates the movie each February. The perfect place to stay is the 1856 Anderson House Hotel, which is Minnesota's oldest hotel. Located one block from the Mississippi River and on Main Street, the Anderson is in the middle of history and close to modern amenities.

Anderson House Hotel
333 Main St., Wabasha, 651-565-2500
theandersonhousehotel.com

Wabasha Chamber of Commerce
122 Main St. W, Wabasha, 651-565-4158
wabashamn.org/chamber-of-commerce

PHOTOGRAPH THE ROUND TOWER
AT FORT SNELLING

Since 1820, the Round Tower has stood tall at Fort Snelling. Originally called Fort St. Anthony, the fort was renamed Fort Snelling in 1825 after Colonel Josiah Snelling, the man who supervised the fort's construction. Fort Snelling served as a recruiting station for the Civil War and three other wars before being closed in 1946. The round and hexagon towers are part of the original lower post, which was restored in the mid-1960s.

The round tower is one of the most photographed buildings on the site. Its limestone exterior rises 25 feet and had slits for muskets to defend the fort. Oddly enough, the round tower was never attacked and its cannons were never shot on the grounds. The musket slits were enlarged to windows. A major site renovation occurred in the early 2020s and resulted in the new Plank Museum and Visitor Center. Admission is purchased at this building. The site is managed by the Minnesota Historical Society and is on the National Register of Historic Places.

200 Tower Ave., St. Paul, 612-726-1171
mnhs.org/fortsnelling

TOUR
THE HISTORIC HENRY SIBLEY HOUSE

Henry Hastings Sibley was Minnesota's first governor and helped shape Minnesota government. From fur trading through the state's early beginnings, the Sibley Historic Site was present in the action. Four limestone buildings still stand (dating from 1825–1853) including the Sibley House and the Dupuis House, which now operates as the gift and souvenir shop. This was Sibley's home estate, the residence where his business and political aspirations took hold. The renovated Sibley House is the oldest private residence in Minnesota.

Guided tours take visitors through the four restored buildings and explain the importance of the site and the man it honors. Self-guided tours take visitors through the grounds and include historical information. The Minnesota Historical Society owns the site; the Dakota County Historical Society manages it.

1357 Sibley Memorial Hwy., Mendota, 651-452-1596
mnhs.org/sibley

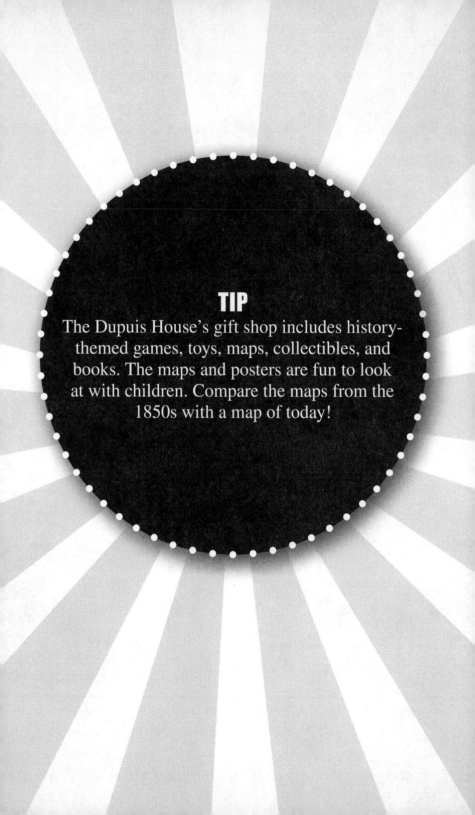

TIP

The Dupuis House's gift shop includes history-themed games, toys, maps, collectibles, and books. The maps and posters are fun to look at with children. Compare the maps from the 1850s with a map of today!

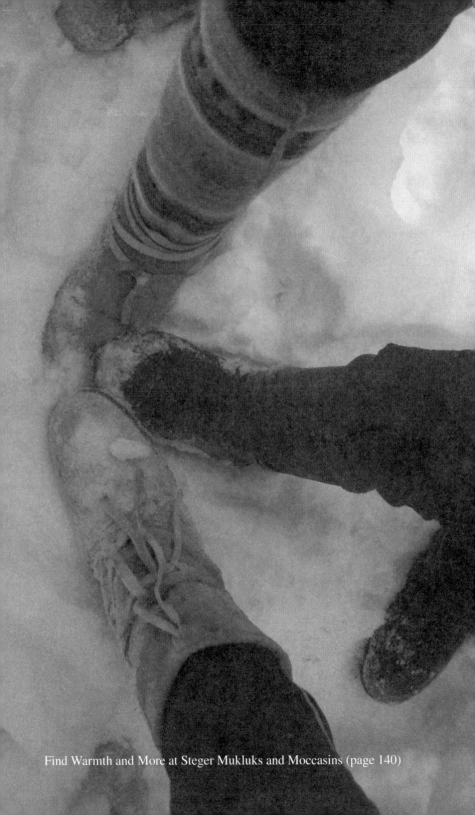

Find Warmth and More at Steger Mukluks and Moccasins (page 140)

SHOPPING
AND FASHION

APPRECIATE ARTISTS
AT THE SHOPPES OF LITTLE FALLS

The Shoppes of Little Falls is a consignment shopper's dream, due to the number of vendors (over 70 at this time), the variety of merchandise, and the tastefully organized floor space. Large street windows allow copious amounts of sunshine to dance on the merchandise, even in winter, creating a joyful shopping experience.

On any given day, you will find hand-embroidered dish towels and aprons, homemade jewelry, handcrafted wood and ceramic kitchen items, paintings, note cards, books by your favorite Minnesota authors, and seasonal items. They even have goodies for pets!

Special events occur multiple times a year. My favorite is the Book Friday, held on what is traditionally known as Black Friday. Minnesota authors gather at the Shoppes of Little Falls, sign their books, and chat with readers. Books make the perfect gift for every occasion.

102 1st St. SE, Little Falls, 320-639-0155
shoppesoflittlefalls.com

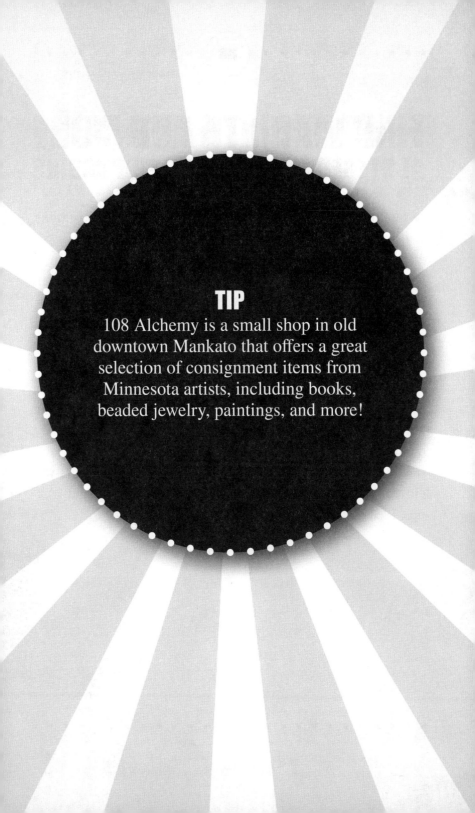

TIP

108 Alchemy is a small shop in old downtown Mankato that offers a great selection of consignment items from Minnesota artists, including books, beaded jewelry, paintings, and more!

FIND WARMTH AND MORE
AT STEGER MUKLUKS AND MOCCASINS

A familiar phrase in Minnesota is that we have two seasons, winter and road construction, both lasting about six months. So, excellent winter footwear is a must for both outdoor enjoyment and running to your car after work. The warmest winter boots in the world are made in Ely at Steger Mukluks and Moccasins. Will Steger wore a pair of Arctic Mukluks on his expeditions to the frozen north and his feet stayed warm and dry. People as far away as Norway agree with Will: these boots are the best.

I love my Steger Mukluks. They are stylish enough for all-day wear in my office, and warm enough for my outdoor adventures. The Steger retail store also sells Chaco sandals, comfortable clothing, boots, accessories, and warm jackets (another necessity). At the time of printing, the retail store was closed, but curbside service was available for fitting and pick-ups. Please call 218-365-6634 for current store hours.

33 E Sheridan St., Ely, 218-365-6634
mukluks.com

DISCOVER
THE WALKER GENERAL STORE

After eating delicious barbecue at Wilbur's on Walker Bay (#4), walk over to the Walker General Store, where you will find just about everything needed for the rest of your vacation. Its old-fashioned vibe is a nice change from busy department malls. From jams and jellies to clothing and footwear, you'll find something fun for everyone. The Walker General Store stocks a great assortment of old-time candy like Razzles and Laffy Taffy to tame the sweet tooth on your ride back to the cabin. They also stock puzzles, card games, and board games to keep the family busy on rainy days.

Walker General Store supports Minnesota small businesses by carrying local books, snacks, and artist wares. Fashion favorites such as Minnetonka Mocs, Minnesota Up North, and Northwoods clothing means that sudden dip in temperatures won't send you packing home early.

420 Minnesota Ave. W, Walker, 218-547-0686
walkergeneralstore.com

CHOOSE WOOL
AT THE BEMIDJI WOOLEN MILLS

First winter in Minnesota? Stop at Bemidji Woolen Mills for the warmth of natural wool to snuggle into. For over 100 years, the Batchelder family has sold high-quality woolen outerwear as well and woolen underwear. From head to toe, inside and out, they have it all. The great benefit of buying quality apparel is that it doesn't go out of style. (Think buffalo plaid jackets.) Year after year, you'll stay warm, dry, and fashionable.

Bemidji Woolen Mills' blankets and throws are a great gift for students heading off to college or newlyweds moving into their first home. Timeless patterns such as the Chief Joseph Blanket (designed in 1920) are always the center of attention in rustic cabins and vacation homes.

301 Irvine Ave. NW, Bemidji, 218-751-5166
bemidjiwoolenmills.com

BEGIN BETTER HEALTH
AT HOLISTIC WELLNESS SERVICES

Education is a key component to the Holistic Wellness Services's mission. This family-owned hemp CBD farm-to-retail-store business grows its own plants just a short distance from their retail store, and then turns the hemp into full-spectrum hemp CBD products. Each plant receives individualized care, which is a quality-control measure, unlike large commercial farms that grow thousands of plants. Products are tested by a lab in Minnesota to ensure THC levels are within state guidelines.

Full-spectrum products include herbal body rub, which aids in pain relief; CBD tinctures that sooth nervous irritability and increase balance naturally; dry skin salve; pet CBD oil; and more. Owners Nate and Breana Crotteau have a trained hemp nurse on staff to answer questions and educate new cannabis users on how their products may interact with people.

499 Arrowhead Ln., Moose Lake, 218-626-7006
hwshemp.life

VISIT LOVE FROM MINNESOTA
IN THE MALL OF AMERICA

Minnesota is home to the largest shopping mall in the United States of America! Without a doubt, it is one of the largest in the world. Imagine 500 stores, over 50 dining establishments, Nickelodeon Universe, Legoland, Sea Life, and more neat places tucked under one roof. It's too much to see in just one day.

Since 1992, the Mall of America (MOA) has welcomed travelers from across the world and helped them experience "Minnesota Nice" firsthand. Weekly specials and community service events further spread Minnesota's generosity to those in need. One fall, over 8,000 backpacks were stuffed with school supplies in just six hours.

Let's face it, the real reason most people visit the MOA is for some serious retail therapy. A super-fun, all-Minnesota shop is Love from Minnesota. Shelf after shelf holds clothing, glassware, gifts, and games that will delight toddlers to grandparents. Pick up a Minnesota Nice sweatshirt to remember your trip.

Love from Minnesota
380 W Market, Level 3, MOA, Bloomington, 952-854-7319
lovefromcompanies.com

FIND "ARTSY"
AT THE HAIRY MOSQUITO TRADING COMPANY

The Hairy Mosquito is a cross between an artist community and a vintage shop(s). It's unique, quirky, and fun for everyone, especially supporters of original art! If you dream it, one of the artists can most likely build it.

Each month starts off with an art show, which gives artists the opportunity to showcase their work. From the leather shop and glass blowing to the silversmith, art abounds. The gem lab has Minnesota's state gem—agates—and many other gem-quality stones from across the world. Visitors can see cut and polished examples of stones in a variety of sizes. See, buy, and create your own art on location, or stop by the trading post or ice cream shop for a snack before you dig into the art. It's hard to shop on an empty stomach.

21287 US Hwy. 169, Milaca, 320-983-5240
hairymosquito.com

LOCATE TREASURES
AT MARINE GENERAL STORE

Marine General Store is the oldest continuously operated general store in Minnesota. The outside of the building looks like it's from the 1800s, and it is! This little treasure is tucked in Marine on St. Croix near the St. Croix River and the William O'Brien State Park. It's the perfect place for hikers and bikers to refuel and stock up on basics such as bread, milk, and eggs.

Marine General goes beyond the basics; they also have gifts, local T-shirts, trinkets, treasures, fishing line, and camping gear. Their full-service deli offers great soups, sandwiches, and specials. Think of them as an old-fashioned service store that can meet all your modern needs.

101 Judd St., Marine on St. Croix, 651-433-2445
marinegeneralstore.com

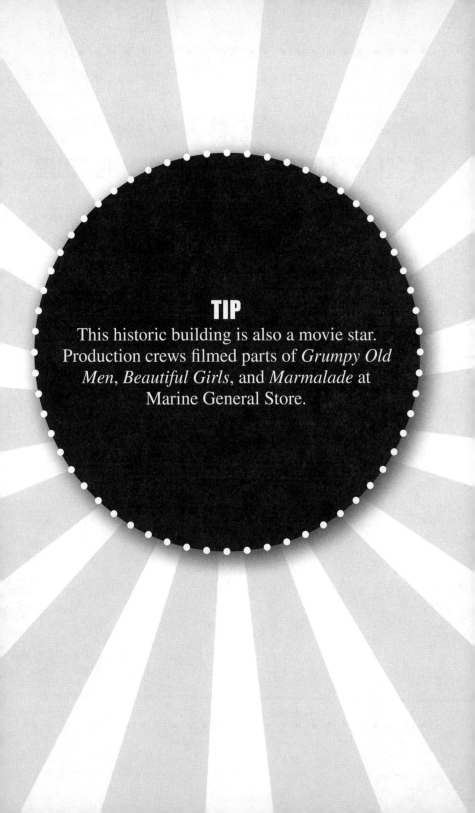

TIP

This historic building is also a movie star. Production crews filmed parts of *Grumpy Old Men*, *Beautiful Girls*, and *Marmalade* at Marine General Store.

TAKE
A MINNESOTA INDIE BOOKSTORE TOUR

Minnesota Independent Bookstore Day is typically held the third Saturday in April. It's a day set aside to show our appreciation for our independent bookstores, and in turn, they offer some sweet store-specific deals. The Midwest Independent Booksellers Association creates a Midwest Indie Bookstore Roadmap every April just before the big day. Each state has a host of independent bookstores highlighted in the full-color guide. These small businesses feature both local and national authors, and many also sell gifts, games, and souvenirs. Keep the map and when traveling, check out your nearest indie bookstore. There are too many great Minnesota independent bookstores to list. A few on the map are listed on the next page.

GRAB FUN
AT VINTAGE VINYL, TOYS, AND GAMES LLC

Vinyl records have made a comeback the last five years, and with their return, so have classic record shops. Vintage Vinyl, Toys, and Games LLC combines lots of neat things to add to your home collection. Vinyl records, check. Action figures, check. Vintage toys, check. Games of all types, check. It's a fun stop for music and movie lovers, comic book followers, and game lovers alike.

Special dollar sales keep merchandise flowing from the shelves. New items are added weekly, so stop by Redwood Falls' only record shop often. If you decide to let your collection of superheroes go, give this place a call before you do anything too wild.

111 E 2nd St., Redwood Falls, 507-627-2889

WALK THROUGH THE GRAND SHOPS
OF KAHLER

The Grand Shops of Kahler are located on the floor below and the floor above the lobby in the Kahler Grand Hotel in Rochester, by the Mayo Clinic. Any trip to the Mayo requires a little stress release. One way to relieve stress is to walk the 65-plus stores and restaurants in the Grand Kahler. Another way is to experience retail therapy by shopping in several of the businesses. A third way to relieve stress is partaking in the special events at the Kahler, whether it's a musical event, large fundraiser, or quaint party, a little laughter and time with friends are a great way to spend the evening.

Shops include medical supplies, eyewear, clothing, art galleries, barber and hair salons, books, and more. With too many stores to list, please check the shop listing on their website. Walking relieves stress; walk through the Grand Shops of Kahler.

20 2nd Ave. SW, Rochester, 800-533-1655
kahler.com/stay-dine-shop

SHOP
THE GRANDE DEPOT

St. Cloud is a fantastic town to take in a few hours of, or to spend a weekend full of, retail therapy. Visitors can find the typical big-box stores and some really interesting small businesses. The Grande Depot in St. Cloud houses both Cork & Cask and Accentric & European: two shops that feature fine wines, spirits, culinary tools and gadgets, and high-quality gourmet foods perfect for social events, romantic evenings, and everyday meals.

Located in the 1912 Eden Valley railroad station, the shops occupy some interesting spaces. The old ticket booth sometimes contains a jewelry display. The owner's office is in the attic of the train station. Unique spaces definitely add to the shopping experience. All aboard for a unique shopping experience.

8318 MN-23, St. Cloud, 320-257-5500
thegrandedepot.com

TIP

Shortly after Halloween, the Grande Depot is decorated for the holiday season. Beautiful decorations and samples are sure to lure in shoppers from the cold.

TRAVEL NORTH
TO THE AMETHYST MINE PANORAMA

This one is a stretch because the Amethyst Mine Panorama isn't actually in Minnesota. If you visited #73, consider this "Thing" an extension of your trip. The Amethyst Mine Panorama is located just east of Thunder Bay across the Minnesota border crossing. You will need an enhanced Minnesota driver's license, pass card, or a passport to travel into Canada. Due to the COVID-19 pandemic, please check ahead for special requirements.

Amethyst's coloring ranges from the lightest lavender to a deep reddish purple. All colors have been found in this mine. After a tour of the mine, you can pick your own stones from the picking field or stroll through the gift shop for an assortment of jewelry, gifts, and loose amethyst rocks. If you choose to pick your own amethyst from the picking field, the mine charges a set price per pound. The sizes, shapes, and colors make the picking field sparkle in the sunshine.

The Lukinuk family runs a large gift shop and lapidary workshop in Thunder Bay.

The Amethyst Mine Panorama
500 Bass Lake Rd., Shuniah, Ontario, 807-622-6908
amethystmine.com

Amethyst Gift Centre
400 E Victoria Ave., Thunder Bay, Ontario

TIP

On your way back to the border, stop at the Pigeon River Provincial Park. There you will see the High Falls from the Canadian side. Once back in Minnesota, the Grand Portage State Park offers a different view of the High Falls. Both views are breathtaking as the Pigeon River falls 120 feet.

BUY QUALITY CLOTHING
AT DULUTH TRADING COMPANY

Minnesota has four seasons, each requiring very different clothing. Duluth Trading Company designs and tests the clothes they create to make sure items hold up to our tough Minnesota standards. We want clothing that climbs the trail with us and other pieces that are soft enough to wear day after day in our offices. We want summer clothes that breathe and winter clothes that keep us warm. Duluth Trading delivers. Their Armachillo and Fire Hose clothing are great examples of quality clothing that lasts.

Clothing is a large part of their inventory; they also sell duffel bags, shoes, purses, camping items, dog gear, and home goods. Shoppers really need to visit a store near them to see the quality and assortment for themselves. Luckily, there are five Duluth Trading Company stores across Minnesota.

Duluth Trading Company
300 E Superior St., Duluth, 218-481-7580
9801 Lyndale Ave. S, Bloomington, 952-884-3561
252 57th Ave. NE, Fridley, 612-255-5201
307 Main St., Red Wing, 651-212-2261
9320 Hudson Rd., Woodbury, 952-225-5410

Finding beauty in winter is easy throughout Minnesota

ACTIVITIES
BY SEASON

WINTER

Enjoy the Igloo Bar at Zippel Bay, 4

Find Warmth and More at Steger Mukluks and Moccasins, 140

Ski Minnesota, 101

See the Northern Lights, 68

Attend the Dragon Festival, 116

See the Clayton, Jackson, and McGhie Memorial, 131

Swim at Flandrau State Park, 70

Light Up Your Evening at Wow! Zone, 58

See the World's Third-Largest Nutcracker Collection
   at the Rock County Historical Center, 130

Chill by the Detroit Lakes Ice Palace, 77

Watch the Dakota 38+2 Wokiksuye Memorial Ride, 114

SPRING

Photograph the Round Tower at Fort Snelling, 133

Grab Lunch at Pedal Pushers Café, 23

Appreciate Mankato's Walking Sculpture Tour, 48

Fish the Northwest Angle, 64

Bike the Paul Bunyan State Trail, 80

Savor Premium Ice Cream, 5

• •

SUMMER

FALL

Count Barn Quilts (page 128)

Stormy Minnesota Skies

SUGGESTED
ITINERARIES

ADULTING

Sip Cold Beer at August Schell Brewing Company, 12

Grab Barbecue at Wilbur's on Walker Bay, 6

Savor Dinner at Owamni by the Sioux Chef, 17

Sample Craft Beer at Small-Town Breweries, 26

Meet the USA 2022 Bartender of the Year at Spoon and Stable, 8

Enjoy a Patio Lunch at Sage on Laurel, 7

Sip Cider at Battle Lake's 1910 Sip House, 30

Enjoy the Igloo Bar at Zippel Bay, 4

Grab Fun at Vintage Vinyl, Toys, and Games LLC, 150

BETTER TOGETHER

Enjoy Multiple Concerts with the Lakes Area Music Festival, 40

Relax at Ely Steam Sauna, 109

Kick Back at Chase on the Lake, 100

Add a Minnesota Wine to Your Dinner, 24

Enjoy Family Time at Sand Lake Resort, 102

Begin Better Health at Holistic Wellness Services, 143

Play Pickleball at River's Edge Park, 72

See the Northern Lights, 68

Zip High with Kerfoot Canopy Tour, 103

• •

RACK UP SOME MILES

YOUTH

· ·

Seppman Mill at Minneopa State Park (page 60)

Crossing Lake Superior to recreate

INDEX

• •

• •

• •

• •

• •

• •

• •

Ken Nyberg Sculpture (page 97)